Native American Encyclopedia of Herbs

The Complete Collection of Herbal Medicine & Natural Remedies to Treat Common Ailments

or How the Ancients' Wisdom Has Kept People Healthy for Centuries

Tallulah Greyeyes

Table of Contents

Introduction

There is a lot of wisdom in ancient traditions and practices, wisdom that often gets forgotten or lost with time, if not preserved and practiced. While people today are mostly reliant entirely on modern medicine, more and more of us are getting discontented with our current state of health and wellbeing. There is medicine available to treat almost any ailment and hurts, but they heal more symptomatically, and often end up causing more health problems than they cure. You often end up getting more side-effects than you bargained for, and instead of making you feel better, these medications end up making you feel a lot worse. You could take a pill for back pain, and end up with an upset stomach. Worst of all, some of these painkillers have addictive properties, which can open up a whole host of issues for the poor unsuspecting victim, who just wanted to stop hurting.

Of course, that is not to say that modern medicine doesn't have its benefits, or that you should swap out modern medicine for alternative treatments entirely, no. However, it doesn't hurt to try natural remedies and recipes for your overall health and wellbeing, so that you feel more energized, more alert and more rejuvenated.

The ancient people had their own remedies and treatments that enabled them to live healthy lives. Even though we are a part of the modern human race, our ways, our diets and our lifestyles have created a whole host of new diseases that didn't even exist in the ancient times. For example, heart disease and diabetes are more prevalent now than it ever was in ancient times, because we have changed the way we eat, our work days are longer, and we barely take the time out for rest. We have now incorporated things into our lifestyles that the human race previously never even consumed. Processed food, sugars, and synthetic drugs are changing our bodies from the inside...little wonder that most of us always end up feeling burnt out and tired.

Consider the story of Desbah, who is a 99 year old Native American woman and is considered to be the very picture of health. She lives a quiet life, tending to her sheep on a lonely little Native American Indian reservation in Arizona. She lives in a modified railroad boxcar, with little to no modern amenities. She doesn't even have modern plumbing or electricity. Yet, she is completely and utterly content. When you see her, you see a petite, good natured woman, with a calming aura around her. Her small home exudes serenity and tranquility, and she greets her guests with graciousness, even though she doesn't get many visitors, apart from her caretaker.

Despite being almost a century old, she is lively and has a sharp mind, and is overall in better health than most people forty years her junior! She has no ailments that afflict the elderly, and apart from aging, doesn't suffer from arthritis or diabetes or any kind of disorders. How has this woman managed to hold on to her health and wellness, almost a century after her birth? How has she managed to not only survive, but live well, without many of the modern amenities that we take for granted?

Many of us have heard of mind over matter before, but this is actually a philosophy for living well. Allopathic systems of care, modern hospitals and doctors determine health by assessing the physical condition of the body, or the mental functionality and capability of the mind. They diagnose ailments based on anything that deviates from their definition of a healthy body, anything different from 'the norm.'

Native Americans on the other hand, believe that health and wellness are intrinsically connected to spirituality. Native Americans basically believe in walking in beauty; a Native American woman puts more stock in having a closer connection to nature and the earth and living harmoniously with the environment. They have their own healing systems and practices, which are effective for them. How else is Desbah the picture of health at the age of 99?

Indigenous healers prescribe a whole host of holistic treatments that are designed to treat a range of acute and chronic conditions, and simply to foster good health and wellbeing. Though these traditions and healing practices differ from tribe to tribe, the core health beliefs are very similar. There are also a multitude of shared traditions and interventional strategies, which include building a healthy foundation, encompassing traditions that deal with a person's physical, psychological, social and spiritual health and wellbeing.

One of the practices that Native Americans swear by, is running each day to 'greet the dawn'. This simple practice is amazingly beneficial; they not only condition the body, but nurture spiritual wellness as well. Stories and legends are passed down in families, as teaching tools to learn good behavior along with what happens if one fails to observe the laws of nature. They are morality tales that foster good values in tribes, communities and families.

This book will tell you about a whole variety of different herbs; it's an encyclopedia of herbalism. You will learn about the healing properties of each herb, how to prepare different herbs to use in the form of potions, poultices and infusions along with many more.

Bon Voyage!

Chapter 1: Native American Medicine

This book briefly touched upon the Native American approach to healing in the introduction, but will elaborate on their philosophies in this section. There is a direct connection between Native American beliefs on religion and health and well-being. Healing is an incredibly spiritual practice for Native Americans; hence they cannot separate healing from the sacred narratives of their culture and religion. Healing ceremonies are an important part of the community experience for many Native Americans. Many researchers that observed various Native American tribes discovered that they could not really distinguish between healing and worship practices. Native American healing ceremonies have the same significance as wearing prayer shawls or other activities of religious reverence. Health to Native Americans is as much a spiritual state of well-being, as it is physical (Lovern & Locust, 2013).

Native Americans firmly believe that a human is a threefold being. In order for a human being to be complete, they need a mind, a body, and a spirit. They believe that the spirit world exists right next to the physical world, and the two worlds intermingle. This ghostly plane is just like the world we live in, less tangible, but every bit as important. They believe that the spirit passes into the spirit world after death as its permanent abode. This stems from the belief that the spirit has always existed; it existed in the spirit world before we were born, and it will remain alive in the spirit world long after our physical bodies have passed away.

Knowing this is important, if you hope to understand how they perceive illness and disease. To indigenous people, illness is not something that debilitates the body alone; it affects your mind and eats away at your spirit as well. Because they so firmly believe that human beings are threefold creatures, they believe that if you want to truly cure an illness, you have to treat the mind, body, and soul alike. Being well, achieving a true state of wellness, means having your mind, body, and spirit working together in perfect harmony. Native American healers treated their patients with this approach; they believed that in order for a body to be well and thrive, the mind, body, and spirit need to be working in harmony with each other, and their holistic treatments reflected this approach.

This practice is now being endorsed by modern science as well. We now know that mental illnesses, such as depression and anxiety, can also physically affect the body. Doctors have now discovered that stress can cause stomach pain, migraines, sleep disorders, and fatigue.

Furthermore, people who suffer from depression can also experience aches and pains throughout their body, along with eye problems and digestive issues.

We have now come to realize the benefits of treating the mind, body, and spirit as well, with many people putting stock in meditation, visualization, breathing techniques, and the power of positive affirmations. We are now realizing what Native Americans have known for years: A person cannot truly be well, unless their mind, body, and spirit are in harmony.

As wellness is achieved when your body, mind, and spirit are in harmony, Native Americans believed you would become unwell if your body, mind, and spirit are in disharmony and cannot align with each other. They believed that we are all responsible for our own wellness, regardless of what has caused us to become unwell. This means that it is up to us to discover what is causing disharmony between our mind, body, and spirit, and then figure out how we can rectify this issue so we can be well again.

Native Americans believed that plants and animals also exist in the spirit world as humans do (Lovern & Locust, 2013). This explains the significance of plants in their lives, and their presence in the spirit world indicates their importance and relevance in their day to day lives. Plants are a source of life; Native Americans used plants and herbs as food and medicine, and as healing and religion go hand in hand, plants have a huge significance in their culture.

Native American Beliefs on Religion and Healing

"Our religion is the tradition of our ancestors—the dreams of our old men and women, given them in the solemn hours of the night by the Great Spirit, and the visions of our tribal chiefs—and is within the heart of our people."—Chief Seattle

There are over two million Native Americans living across the United States and Canada. However, they do not have one uniform religion. They do share similar beliefs, and many keep their ancient beliefs, while some mingle modern Christian beliefs with their own. As there are numerous tribes and communities, they all have their own variations in beliefs. However, some beliefs are uniform and are followed by all Native Americans.

Native Americans don't have any holy books or churches, nor do they have any central figures like Jesus, Moses, or Muhammad. Theirs is an oral tradition that is passed down each generation, based on values and guiding principles that are taught to each child. They grow up internalizing these values and principles, and they become an integral part of each person's life. Those who follow the sacred way do not divide their lives in segments; they see it as one.

They believe in one Great Spirit (a great source of energy that has created everything and binds all creation to itself). It has many names in different tribes and communities, but all agree that it is a great power that is part of all creation. The Great Spirit is in the water, the wind, the trees, the plants, stones, sky, friends, and strangers. It is too great to be imagined in human form because it is considered to be an uncontainable, universal source of energy which is attuned to all of nature, including human nature.

Understanding this is important if you hope to understand the Native American approach to healing. As they believe the Great Spirit is in nature, plants, trees, and humans—you can see how they would see all things as interconnected in their approach to healing.

In Native American culture, shamans, medicine men and women, singers and healers, are all considered to be blessed by the Great Spirit. It is believed that the Great Spirit has bestowed a special gift upon these healers so that they can act as mediators between the spirit world and the earthly plane for the purpose of healing, to renew the spirit, and benefit the community as a whole.

Native American Healthcare

We can learn a lot from Native American beliefs in medicine and healthcare. As mentioned before, health and wellness for Native Americans relies on taking the proper actions and interacting well with the spirit world. If your mind, body, and spirit are not in harmony, you would find yourself feeling unwell. If you hope to achieve a true state of wholeness and wellness, you would need to walk in harmony with the forces of nature and the universe. When you fall out of step with these forces, you would find yourself unhappy and unwell.

We can interpret this in a modern way and see how it applies to our own lives. Maslow's hierarchy of needs states that after our basic physiological needs are met, after we have food, clothing, and shelter, human beings most crave a sense of safety, feeling loved, a sense of belonging, having esteem, respect, and recognition and most of all, the desire to become the most we can be. When any of these needs are not met, we feel unhappy, unfulfilled, and unmotivated.

When we are taking care of our physiological needs, we end up nourishing our body. We eat good food and have refreshing drinks, we breathe fresh air, and we wear comfortable clothes and sleep in soft, warm, beds. We have a roof over our heads to protect us from the elements and we make physical connections with other human beings for pleasure and to reproduce. If we take away any of these things from our lives, can we be happy? Can we be content? Can we even survive?

We seek security in the form of employment, education, and by gathering resources and property. We nourish our minds through learning, by becoming strong, by making our place in this world and forming an identity. We build up our image to get recognition; we strive to achieve a sense of accomplishment and self-esteem.

Lastly, we make friends, we fall in love, and we make meaningful connections with others to nourish our spirit. We try to be the very best versions of ourselves so that we can feel happy from within, instead of aligning our happiness with external sources.

If any of these things fall out of balance, we fall out of balance. Our lives become disharmonious; we end up messing up different aspects of our lives. For example, if someone is going through a breakup or a divorce, they deal with a myriad of different, strong, and debilitating emotions. One can experience depression, anxiety, insomnia, and heartache. When your mind is preoccupied with something, it's really hard to concentrate on other areas of your life. Someone going through a breakup might end up falling behind at work, or neglecting their household chores because the harmony of their lives has become disrupted.

What we have discovered fairly recently, that mental health plays a role in determining your overall physical health and wellness, Native Americans have believed for centuries. They believe that illness is caused when a person falls out of step with natural forces. To them, being well means being able to walk in harmony with nature; failure or inability to do so results in an overall state of sickness.

Native Americans doctors and healers seek to treat the body as a whole, instead of just treating a patient symptomatically, like most western doctors. Native American healers try to identify the elements that are causing the patient to fall out of harmony in their lives. They consider the spirit to be equally as important to the body, and in order to heal the body properly, the spirit has to be well.

Keeping this in mind, a Native American with a broken arm might seek help from a doctor or physician to treat their injury, but also would refer to a traditional medicine man or medicine woman to take care of the spirit that is suffering as well.

C. Locust (1988) wrote an article entitled "Wounding the spirit, Discrimination and traditional American Indian belief systems." It states that Native Americans believe that in order to treat and heal a patient suffering from a broken leg, a medicine man or woman would start by treating the spirit, by trying to determine why the broken arm occurred in the first place. They would try to understand the event in a spiritual context, as opposed to a physical one, and then start to affect the process of change, in the mind, body, and spirit, trying to figure out what the cause of the disharmony was that caused the arm to break in the first place.

Most traditional indigenous people believe that illnesses are not just products of the natural world, but are also brought about by supernatural forces. Different tribes have different beliefs about the supernatural, which are reflected in their healing techniques and methods.

For example, the Cherokee believe illnesses are caused by animal spirits that are disrespected by hunters. You can see how closely they revere nature and believe in being gentle with the spirit for them to foster this belief. Other indigenous tribes believe that you get sick as a consequence of your own bad actions. This is kind of like the principle of Karma: The good you do in this world rewards you, and the bad comes back to make you suffer.

The Iroquois tribe believes that human sickness is caused when our desires and dreams remain unfulfilled. They feel unfulfilled—desires weaken and sicken the spirit. The Inuit believe that we can get sick as punishment, to pay for the sins committed by our ancestors. Talk about having a heavy load to bear! Almost all tribes believe that you can also get sick due to the malicious intentions of evil spirits, and have many warding spells and rituals to protect oneself against the malice of evil spirits.

Native Americans also believe that serious and chronic illnesses can be caused by a phenomenon called "soul loss." This occurs when evil spirits, especially those belonging to the dead, end up capturing a sick person's soul while it leaves their body as the person sleeps. You have to be seriously sick in order to get diagnosed with soul loss. You could be in a coma, or be delirious or have a wasting disease.

However, they also have cures for all of these afflictions. Most of these rituals are based on reestablishing the foundation of a person's relationship with nature and spirit world and the interconnected nature of life.

Native Americans consider healers to be sacred and healing and medicine is considered to be a sacred calling. They believe that healing is a gift granted by the Great Spirit to a select few. If one is called into the healing vocation, they must dedicate their lives to honoring that gift. Native American healers use natural means and healing places to cure people who are sick. They believe that the natural forces of the earth bestow healing powers to their healers, which they can access through rituals and prayer.

Native Americans often consider healers, shamans, and medicine men and women to be holy, because they believe healing cannot take place without the assistance and guidance of their Creator. Many modern Native Americans to this day, use a combination of traditional healing ceremonies and modern medicine to stay healthy and well.

Native American Healing and Medicinal Practices

Native Americans have their own traditional healing rituals and medicinal practices. However, most Native Americans these days have adapted to modern medicine, and tolerate and incorporate it into their lives, on their own terms and in their own way.

Native Americans prescribe to their own set of beliefs regarding healing, so while they will accept mainstream medical care, they make sure to bring their own elements and traditions in as well, so that they are staying true to their culture and religion. There are some general practices that all Native Americans share, while other practices can vary from tribe to tribe, and individual to individual.

Native Americans really put a lot of stock into "walking in beauty," one of their main principles of life. This is especially apparent in the Navajo tradition. They include this concept in their prayers as well, and use it as a respectful phrase when they say goodbye. Walking in beauty does not mean walking around beautiful things, or looking beautiful. Beauty, to Native Americans, means living in balance. When they say balance, they refer to a circle which includes our parts as a human. It means our body, mind, heart, and soul. This is just one circle.

Other circles of beauty could include community: family, tribe, plants, animals, brothers, and sisters. A circle of beauty could also refer to the elements: earth, water, wind, and fire. The shared element in all of these is balance; Native Americans believe in maintaining oneness between all parts, a unity, at all costs. The ultimate balance is believed to be between our traditional spiritual self and the universe.

Whenever any of these elements fall out of balance, that is when Native Americans believe sickness occurs. In the time of illness, a doctor might fix the symptom, but does not address the trauma the rest of the body and the mind go through. A Native American healer will aim to fix that, to restore the balance, so that the patient is able to walk in beauty again.

Native Americans have their own medical practices, and allow modern ones under certain circumstances. For example, most indigenous people allow blood transfusions, except the Navajos. The Navajos do not believe in mixing blood, lest it affect the spirit. Most tribes also allow organ transplantation, both donating and receiving organs as well. Navajos do not allow organ transplantation on the same principle (Metropolitan Chicago Healthcare Council [MCHC], n.d.).

Native Americans firmly believe that life is sacred; however, each tribe carries its own beliefs on abortion. The indigenous people do not believe in letting the body linger on in a vegetative state if the patient is on a ventilator and kept alive through artificial means. They do not prolong a person's passing, because of their strong beliefs in the spirit world. They have certain prayers that are meant to be recited in front of their family and tribe when someone passes. The indigenous people also generally don't consent to getting autopsied because they believe that causes further trauma to the human body and spirit. They don't like causing the body or spirit any more harm than strictly necessary. However, if it is a legal issue, then they do relent (MCHC, n.d.).

Even though Native Americans are fairly advanced in the usage of herbal medicine, they do not readily accept synthetic medication into their bodies. They are not opposed to it, but are hesitant before taking them. Some indigenous people might try to downplay their pain or deny it because they do not like accepting that their bodies are failing them (MCHC, n.d.). They value strength, and to them beauty is balance, so to admit pain and weakness, is accepting that they are out of balance with nature.

Native American patients also fear getting addicted to medicine, or having reactions to them. Again, because these medicines are synthetic, they are wary of using them. They also don't like taking synthetic medication because they believe that if they are dying, they need to meet their Creator with a clear mind. Some Native Americans also don't like modern medication because they so staunchly believe that their Creator will heal them using the traditional healing methods of their people (MCHC, n.d.).

Many Native American healing practices include spiritual care in combination with physical healing. They have certain sacred objects, used for healing, or used in their healing traditions to help expedite or facilitate the healing process.

Native Americans use what is called a medicine bundle, or a medicine bag for healing. A medicine bag is a collection of objects that hold sacred meaning and spirit power. These are usually wrapped up in cloth, or are made out of animal skin. All of these items hold special significance and are connected to creation in some way. The bag could hold things like crystals, stones, shells, feathers, and tobacco (MCHC, n.d.).

Medicine bundles or bags could be owned by individuals or could be the joint property of a clan or a tribe. These bundles are considered sacred, and are meant to be treated with reverence and respect. If a Native American person gives a medicine bag to someone for safekeeping, that is considered a sacred duty; it must be executed with solemn responsibility and considered to be a great honor (MCHC, n.d.).

There are other objects from different tribes that are considered to be sacred and hold immense spiritual significance. For example, the sacred pipe of the Lakota. The pipe holds great religious significance, and is carved by items that hold special meaning. Each part symbolizes the Native American connection with each part of the world. The stem of the pipe signifies their connection with plants; the bowl, their connection with animals. The tobacco in the pipe symbolizes their relationship with other humans, with the breath that goes into the pipe representing the elements on earth. Finally, the smoke emitting from the pipe signifies spiritual beings ("Sacred Pipe," n.d.).

The Pueblo people of the Southwest have Paho; sacred prayer sticks that they prepare meticulously by carving and decorating them with shells, stones, and feathers. The Hopi and Huron make masks that they were in sacred dances. Some Native Americans use sacred herbs for rituals, such as using tobacco, sweet grass, and sage for purification. They use feathers and the medicine wheel to lift up their prayers, and medicinal plants and herbs are considered to be special gifts bestowed to us by the spirit world to heal people who are sick. They know about more than four hundred different species of wild plants and herbs that they use as medicine effectively.

They have many rituals that they use as a part of their healing traditions.

The indigenous people have long standing purification rituals where sage, cedar, and sweet grass is used to cleanse impurities from a particular area, or from a person's aura. The process of smudging involves letting smoke that emits from burning specific herbs spread all over a person or a place. All the areas that the smoke touches are considered to be purified.

The smoke is significant because it is believed that it can carry all the prayers back to the creator as it blows in the wind. Native American healers often use feathers and fans in these rituals to help spread the smoke. Sometimes these rituals need to happen indoors. If such is the case, to avoid fire hazards, the dried herbs in smudge sticks are replaced with oils instead. These are simply essential oils made from the same herbs, substituted for smoke (MCHC, n.d.).

The indigenous people also use Tobacco ties as sacred objects. Tobacco ties are basically small bundles of tobacco wrapped up in cloth. They give these items to friends, as a sign of their friendship. They are also sometimes strung on a tree branch to carry prayers. The process of making these objects is important, as making them is believed to be an act of worship.

Native Americans also have feather ceremonies. In a feather ceremony, a sick person would lie down as a healer sweeps their body with feathers. They can also have feathers tied to their body, or they can be made to handle feathers as well. The feathers are items with cleansing power; they 'sweep' away illnesses and impurities. They heal the person holistically, preparing them for a new lease on life and also opening them up for supernatural intervention in a positive way.

Face painting is also a sacred ritual for Native Americans. If a person is seriously ill and needs surgery, or at death's door, they would get their faces painted. They also paint faces of the dead, as a ritual to protect the body after the soul passes on. They use healing herbs and oils along with roots for emotional and spiritual healing as well, along with treating the body for physical ailments.

Native Americans also use fetishes; objects that represent the power of the spirits of animals that help in healing the sick. They use these objects to feel strong; they are considered to be a source of power and strength. These totems are not only believed to be symbolically strong, but Native Americans believe they can actually help you feel better after being weak from sickness.

A pipe ceremony is a healing ceremony performed by a Native American spiritual healer. It is up to the patient where the ceremony is performed. Sometimes a sick person would want this ceremony to take place right in the hospital. Mostly it takes place in a traditional setting. It basically involves the healer smoking a special pipe with the patient. Since hospitals these days don't allow smoking, the patient is allowed sometimes to leave the premises to do so. If the doctor doesn't think that's a good idea, the healer could also ask the doctor to pray over the pipe with the patient, then they would go smoke it elsewhere.

Music plays an important role in Native American healing traditions. They use drums and rattles and pair them with Chantways and songs. This is a normal part of healing traditions for many indigenous people. Tribal singers are invited to sing traditional songs for the sick. This is considered to be an emotionally healing process.

Each sound is symbolic; drums stand for the beating heart, belonging to us and the mother earth. The rattling sound of the shaker is reminiscent of medicinal ceremonies. When a person is in a coma, close to death, they end up losing most of their senses. The sound of music is meant to be comforting; familiar sounds that connect them to loved ones—a simplistic way of reminding the patient they are not alone in their time of passing.

Another important healing tradition that Native Americans believe in is the Medicine Lodge. Also known as an Inipi lodge, it is where purification ceremonies take place. This place is also called a sweat lodge. The patient goes inside an enclosed area to get purified. There, they are exposed to intense heat. This is done to stimulate our insight and enhance our powers of vision. The sweat lodge also has known medical benefits as it detoxifies the body, stimulates blood flow, and compels the body to sweat out any impurities and toxins.

A traditional Medicine Lodge is shaped like a dome. It is a round shed, built quite low, close to the ground. They fill it with steam which emits from rocks heated just outside the lodge. These heated rocks are brought inside, placed in the center using a shovel inside a pit already dug in that area. As the rocks cool, they get replaced with hotter rocks. This traditionally is done in four rounds; the lodge keeps getting hotter with the more rocks that are added, filling up with steam.

The ceremony is led by a healer. They "pour the water," which is considered to be an important step in the ceremony. It is the healer's job to ensure the wellness of everybody involved in the ritual. Usually this takes place in a group setting with the maximum of a dozen people. The healer doesn't directly pour the water on the participants; the water is poured on the hot rocks to give off steam.

They also cover the rocks in fragrant herbs such as sage or sweet grass. This is done to create aromatic smoke. Aromatherapy is known to have healing results; these herbs are meant to cleanse and relax.

The participants might also be smudged with smoke from sage sticks before entering the lodge. During the ceremony, the participants are encouraged to pray and discuss their innermost thoughts and feelings to heal better. They might also be asked to pray to the Creator to purge their lives from sickness, pain, and suffering (Brown, 2019).

Sweat lodges are considered to be quite beneficial for the mind, body, and soul, and many indigenous people can opt for this before undergoing surgery or any other serious medical procedure. A person might also get a healer to pray on their behalf if they don't feel up to doing it themselves.

Most people are aware that crystals and sacred stones are significant objects for Native Americans. These objects are arranged onto a person's body or are held while a person prays. These crystals are often placed in four different directions during prayer, as a substitute for the sacred pipe.

Like many other religions and cultures, Native Americans also believe in the benefits of fasting. Native Americans believe fasting heals a spirit that is lacking harmony. It is by no means mandatory and people who are sick are never advised to fast. In Native American culture, you can also fast on another person's behalf if they can't do it themselves. Fasting is attributed to many positive effects such as detoxification, cleansing, and healing the body.

Native Americans also have sacred foods that are a part of their healing traditions. These foods range from specially brewed teas or recipes created using sacred herbs to help a sick person heal faster and feel better (MCHC, n.d.).

These are just a few of the Native American healing and medicinal practices and beliefs. As mentioned before, their beliefs and practices vary from tribe to tribe and individual to individual. Now that we know a little bit about them, we can discuss how Native American Medicine can be incorporated in our modern lives as well.

Chapter 2: Incorporating Native American Medicine in Our Modern Lives

As mentioned in a previous chapter, medicine, healthcare, and religion go hand in hand in Native American culture. Even though most of their ancient practices have modernized over time, some tribes still keep to the old ways and practice the same beliefs they did hundreds of years ago. Historically, healthcare in Native American tribes has been grounded in the concept of balance. They picture a truly healthy person as somebody who has balance in every aspect of their lives. As mentioned earlier, Native Americans believe that in order for a person to be whole, their physical, mental, spiritual, and social selves need to be in sync. They do not attribute ailments to just physical pathology, but they think being unwell is a state brought about by an imbalance of these components.

As they subscribe to these beliefs, many tribes understood ailments as something that could be brought about by natural causes or supernatural cases as well, and their treatment practices reflected ways that dealt with both aspects.

Native Americans have ancient health care practices. We never know exactly how far they date back as they never wrote anything down. Instead, these traditions were passed down generation by generation through stories and apprenticeships. Europeans came to America in the 16th century; before that nobody wrote any of their traditions and healing rituals down. Besides, indigenous healers never wanted to share their secrets with invaders as this knowledge was sacred and they didn't earn the right to learn it ("Native American Medicine," n.d.).

Native American Medicine is exceptionally hard to understand, especially for outsiders. They use a lot of herbalism in their healing techniques, which varies, can be adapted according to tribe and circumstance, and can be tweaked as per the healer's preference. This makes it difficult for outsiders to replicate or record as a typical piece of medicinal work. Records throughout history can only depict a portion of a certain healing practice performed at a specific time, but it does not apply to Native American medicine as a whole. Still, just because it's difficult, doesn't mean it's impossible. People have observed and learned from these practices to identify trends and patterns which have then been documented ("Native American Medicine," n.d.).

Indigenous people believe in the philosophy of connecting humanity and nature with the spiritual realm. A modern doctor only seeks to cure a person's ailments symptomatically, while an indigenous healer examines their patient's lives and their relationships with other people along with their physical health. They then devise a personalized, holistic method of treatment. This might include a combination of healing techniques, involving herbalism, ceremony, singing, praying, and sweating.

Introduction to New World Science

When the colonizers from Europe set foot in the Americas and started uneasily living side by side with the indigenous people, they brought their own technologies to the New World, which the natives had never heard of before. However, it is unwise to categorize the Natives as primitive savages that were colonized by the sophisticated Europeans. In fact, Native Americans have contributed immensely from science and the colonizers ended up learning quite a lot from them as well.

Food science is one of the best examples. Since the Native Americans lived off the land and had a very deep, spiritual relationship with nature, they were fairly advanced in horticulture and food science in ways the Europeans had never learned before. It was the Native

Americans who figured out how to cultivate and breed some of the most economically important foods that we consume today. They were pioneers in growing corn, beans, potatoes, and peanuts, amongst many others.

We might think that these vegetables had been available to the Europeans in their homelands as well, but that was far from the case. For instance, corn was very valuable to the indigenous people; they equated its yellow gleam with gold. However, traditionally, the original plant from which corn was grown was a wild plant that was only capable of growing near the equator. It was the indigenous people of America that figured out how to grow modern varieties of corn through centuries of meticulous hybridization and selection. This is why we now enjoy several varieties of corn that can grow in numerous climates. We got that knowledge from the Native Americans.

Similarly, modern science learned a lot about medicine from Native American culture as well. They were surprisingly medically advanced for their time, and their medical systems were complex. Their healers used narcotics, anesthetics, enemas, psychotherapy and many other modern medical practices long before they became commonplace in modern medicine. Native American healers especially contributed to modern medicine.

They discovered Quinine to treat malaria, perhaps because of their close proximity to nature, and Ipecac as well, an agent used to induce vomiting to treat poisoning. It was the Native Americans that figured out means for inducing vomiting through chemical means to purge the system from toxins. They also discovered Curare. Modern science now uses Curare derivatives as anesthetics, and the Native Americans were using it to anesthetize their patients long before modern doctors discovered its use.

Role of Native American Healing Traditions in Allopathic Medicine

Even though many people believe that Native American healing traditions are rooted more in spirituality, hence it is a little too esoteric for their taste, there are a lot Native American traditions that have contributed to allopathic medicine. The Native American approach to understanding the human body and what causes it to become unwell, is one that modern medicine is finally starting to grasp. Modern medicine has always taken a very mechanistic view of the human body. Modern doctors believe that illnesses are caused when parts of our body suffer and consider the body to be a sum of parts rather than as a complicated whole. Native Americans take a completely different approach in their beliefs.

They believe that the body is whole, and if even one element of the parts that make it whole is ailing, the entire being suffers. Modern understanding of medicine is a little more complex than that, and Native Americans now incorporate elements of modern medicine and technology into their own traditional beliefs through integration, but still hold on to their traditional beliefs to maintain their cultural autonomy.

The real strength of Native American medicine lies in their knowledge of herbs. They have perfected herblore over centuries of tedious discovery, trial and error, and understand natural remedies perhaps better than any other people in the world. Modern medicine has benefited immensely from the knowledge of herbs that was discovered by Native Americans, learning a lot about their properties and medicinal purposes, and using those to advance allopathic medicine today. Studies depict that over 120 drugs prescribed by doctors today were first created using extracts from plants. They also show that over 75 percent of these drugs were created after studying plants that have commonly been used in Native American Medicine (Smith, 2017).

A few examples include Cascara Sagrada, official name *Rhamnus purshiana,* a common laxative still used in medicine today, along with Dogbane, also known as *Apocynum androsaemifolium,* which is used to treat edema, secondary to kidney and heart failure. Dogbane is also used as an oral contraceptive in modern medicine, as well as in Native American traditions.

They also discovered Foxglove derived from *Digitalis purpurea,* a vital ingredient in medicine meant to treat heart failure. Native Americans used Guaiacum, *Guaiac officinale.* It is actually an antitussive, meant to treat coughs and colds, with the modern name Robutussin. It was also used to conduct a Guaiacum based fecal occult blood test for the indigenous people, but that practice is confined to indigenous communities only.

However, modern medicine still benefits from the Native American practice of using Salicin *(Salix nigra)* to metabolize salicylic acid. This is a revolutionary discovery and has benefitted the modern world as it is the main ingredient used in aspirin. They also used Sassafras *(Sassafras albidum)* as an anthelmintic; meaning it is used to kill parasitic worms that invade our body. It also prevents blood from coagulating along with diarrhea and stops people from vomiting and feeling nauseous (Smith, 2017).

All Native American healers knew a lot about herbal medicine. They knew about the healing properties of each herb and can use specific ones to treat a range of ailments. They were surprisingly advanced for their time, considering they lived in such a primitive age. They were able to fashion syringes out of bones to give injections to their sick. They could also perform complicated medical procedures, such as arthrocentesis, meant to remove synovial fluid that gets accumulated between bone joints. This is a particularly complex procedure even today; it is a thing of wonder that the indigenous people managed to do this effectively without causing long term complications for the patient.

Native Americans also knew how to perform surgery and do wound debridement. Basically this means that when tissue dies around a wound after surgery, doctors remove the unhealthy or dead tissue so that fresh skin can grow in that place. This complicated process is done using lasers or modern scalpels today, but Native Americans were practicing this much long before lasers even were an idea in science fiction.

Native American healers were also skilled at treating conditions of the bones. They knew how to perform complex orthopedic procedures such as tractions and countertraction, along with thoracentesis that removes fluid trapped in larger parts of bone. They also knew how to perform trephination (Smith, 2017).

Trephination is an ancient form of brain surgery. There were hardly any ancient races that would, or could, operate on the brain. The Inca and the Mayans were the exceptions, apart from Native Americans. Trephination is also known as trepanning or burr holing. It is performed basically by drilling a hole into the skull using simple surgical tools. Some healers also incised or scraped their way into the skull, using basic tools. This was an incredibly complicated and difficult procedure and fatal if not done right.

They performed it by drilling a hole into the skull and removing a piece of bone. This way the brain is exposed without damaging any blood vessels or brain matter. It was traditionally used to treat people who suffered from migraines, epilepsy, and mental disorders. Trepanning was also performed as a primitive type of emergency intervention surgery, where they would remove bits of shattered bone from a head that had been caved in or wounded. They would remove the bits of broken bone from the fractured skull and clean out the waterfall of blood that would pool underneath the skull. Modern science actually used trepanning as inspiration for lobotomies that were performed on the mentally ill in later years. Trepanning was also called the medieval lobotomy.

European doctors coming to the New World were awestruck when they discovered these procedures. They were shocked, not only at how effective these procedures were compared to their own, but also that these procedures were much more humane than the ones they were used to following. Even though initially the indigenous people were reluctant to share their healing secrets with the colonizers, they eventually did (Smith, 2017).

European doctors were floored to discover that Native Americans had several effective anesthetics, something that they themselves were severely lacking. In fact, before they discovered these herbal anesthetics, many European doctors resorted to knocking out their patients by punching them, often in the jaw. Other less violent ones used alcohol, ether, or opium. These weren't always effective either, as patients had to be administered massive doses, which often ended up killing the patients.

Native Americans that lived toward Mexico used to administer peyote to patients suffering from lacerations to quell the pain, along with those who suffered from fractured and snakebites. Peyote is such an effective painkiller that many surgeons in the US army adopted it as an official painkiller to be used on soldiers. Native Americans also took peyote to treat mental illness.

Jimson weed, officially known as Jamestown weed or *Datura stramonium*, was also used as an anesthetic taken both externally and internally by the indigenous population of the Virginia area. They ground the roots into a poultice and kept that on skin for external use, or ingested it for a more concentrated effect. Early colonial doctors also adopted this practice because it was a heck of a lot better than socking people in the jaw (Smith, 2017).

Colonial doctors were quick to observe how fastidious Native American healers were when it came to treating complex ailments. They learned their techniques and adopted several of their plant based medicines and were amazed to find how effective these methods were compared to their own. One of the best known examples of this is when French explorer Jacques Cartier was in Canada with his crew, overwintering in what is now called Quebec City. At the time, the place was known as Stadacona, and he decided to wait the winter out there with his crew, mainly because a lot of them were sick and suffering from scurvy. The local Haudenosaunee (indigenous tribe) saved their lives by bringing them a coniferous tree and showing them how to use it to make medicine.

They also taught them several other important treatments, such as using latex from the common dandelion to treat warts, and drinking the fragrant pineapple weed as medicinal tea. Cartier's crew was so grateful at their intervention, that they started calling the coniferous tree the Tree of Life.

After the Europeans came in and settled into the Americas, they bought with them diseases that were previously unheard of amongst the indigenous people. Even then, despite concocting these diseases from the colonial settlers, Native Americans were still able to come up with new healing methods to treat these alien diseases.

Before the Europeans settled in, diseases like smallpox, measles, tuberculosis, and several venereal diseases were unheard of in the Americas, but the Europeans brought these diseases in massive quantities. Things got so bad that these diseases spread to pandemic proportions. The indigenous people utilized their knowledge of herbs to treat some of these afflictions with existing medication, while for others, they worked at concocting new medicines to treat the new ailments symptomatically and as a whole.

They discovered that they can use sweetflag to treat smallpox. Sweetflag was already being used as a medicinal plant meant to treat rashes and things of that nature, and the indigenous people discovered that it was effective at treating smallpox as well. They used q'emiln, officially known as *Barestem lomatium*, to treat tuberculosis. It was so effective that European doctors incorporated it into their treatment plans immediately, calling the herb *Indian Consumption Plant*—meaning that it was used to treat consumption, a common term for Tuberculosis.

As indigenous people started integrating more with the Europeans and started to consume foods that were rich in starch and sugar, diabetes started to become more and more prevalent amongst their people. They discovered traditional medicine for that as well, using the inner bark of devil's club, classified as *Oplopanax horridus*, a shrub which is a part of the ginseng family, *Araliacaeae*.

There is little doubt about the contributions of indigenous people to the field of modern medicine. We can thank them for coming up with humane versions of the barbaric treatment plans that European physicians were previously resorting to, having little knowledge of herbalism or spirituality. It is because they walk in beauty with nature, and have such reverence for all things natural, that they were able to painstakingly discover different herbs and their properties, and apply them so effectively in medicine. Their contributions are significant to the way allopathic medicine is developed today.

Traditional Remedies That Are Healing Us Today

Remedies are passed down as integral knowledge within families and communities, so we could be practicing healing techniques that our ancestors discovered hundreds of years ago. The reason why these remedies stand the test of time is because they really do work, and they really are effective. We should treasure these remedies as the wisdom of our ancestors, passed down generations, to keep us happy, healthy, and safe.

The proof speaks for itself. Thanks to modern technology, we are now rediscovering the secrets of the earth and the universe that became lost to us over the years as the world moved on. Just recently, one of the winners of the Nobel Prize of medicine, Dr. Tu Youyou, discovered a breakthrough medicine after studying over 2,000 ancient herbal remedies and recipes. Dr. Youyou discovered artemisinin, an anti-malarial drug that is derived from wormwood, something indigenous people had been using for hundreds of years. Dr. Youyou won the Nobel Prize for medicine because this discovery has enabled doctors to save millions of lives that were otherwise lost due to malaria. The answer wasn't something new; it lay in something old, secrets of the ancient peoples forgotten in the modern world.

The miracles of ancient herbs being rediscovered to heal the modern world aren't just limited to wormwood. Digoxin taken from foxgloves is used to treat heart failure and also helps the heart to beat with a more regular rhythm. We recently rediscovered this, when foxglove had been used as a traditional healing method by indigenous people for a very long time.

Opium in poppies was originally discovered in Mesopotamia, spreading throughout Asia where its use was rampant amongst the ancient civilizations. Opium came to the west in 1527, and was a widespread remedy for many medications ranging from sleeping aids to cough medication and painkillers. It was only made illegal in the 19th century after its addictive properties were discovered. Still, without the discovery of opium, we would not have many opiate based painkillers which are so essential to medicine today. Without opium, we would not have morphine, a powerful painkiller given to patients to help treat the pain after surgery and painful injuries.

Quinine is another ancient herb that is considered a gem from the past that has contributed immensely to modern medicine. Quinine comes from the cinchona tree, and is used to treat malaria to this day. Modern science has recognized the importance of traditional medicine now; in fact we have now dedicated an entire branch of science to unearthing ancient healing secrets and studying traditional medicine, called ethnopharmacology.

Many people think that getting medicine from plants is as simple as extracting the essence of a plant, or isolating its active ingredients, but actually it's a long and complicated process, full of hazards. That is why it is so amazing that our technologically deprived ancestors figured out ways of using these plants safely as medicine. Fact is, a lot of these medicinal plants are poisonous in their raw form. If you want to convert these plants into medication, you need to learn how to extract the useful ingredients from the poisonous matter, and for that we would need a lot of meticulous procedures and an abundance of raw material.

Modern scientists have to work hard to develop strategies to carefully perform these measures, and the fact that our ancestors were able to do this with limited equipment and self-taught knowledge, is amazing indeed.

We still use a lot of traditional remedies to heal ailments we face in our lives today. Here are a few examples:

Milkweed

Milkweed is called such because it excretes a milky white sap. This white sap is also called petty spurge. Sap from milkweed has been used as a treatment for warts since 1826. We need to be careful using raw milkweed though because it can also irritate the skin.

However, people have been growing milkweed in their homes and gardens for years, using it to treat warts and sunspots as well. Milkweed was officially incorporated in modern medicine in 1997, when Dr. Aylward isolated ingenol mebutate, its active ingredient, from the rest of the plant because he discovered that it was toxic. It would deteriorate rapidly replicating human tissue. Once the dangerous aspect of the herb was identified, it was discovered that milkweed sap is also excellent at preventing lesions from turning into skin cancer. A perfect example of how a gem from the past turns into lifesaving medical knowledge in the future.

Leeches

Whenever we think of leeches being used in medical procedures, we immediately conjure images of medieval times with screaming patients shivering in horror as big, fat leeches are placed on their bodies to suck up their blood. Or maybe if you're a pop culture fan, you immediately thought of *Game of Thrones*, where Lord Bolton was an ardent fan of leeching as it "removes all the bad blood and keeps a person calm." Regardless of how you've heard about it, we all are aware of leeches being used in medicine for a very long time.

Many of us would be surprised to know, however, that the practice of leeching did not die out in medieval times. Modern doctors have recently rediscovered the benefits of using leeches as a healing technique.

In ancient times, leeching was considered to be one of the more sophisticated and civilized methods of bloodletting. Bloodletting was one of the most common cures for many diseases, from fevers to upset stomachs, to mental illness.

Ancient Greeks believed that disease was caused by an imbalance in any of the four bodily 'humors.' These humors were blood, phlegm, black bile, and yellow bile. This belief was originated by ancient Greek physician Hippocrates, after whom the modern Hippocratic Oath is named today.

Much like the indigenous people, the Greeks also believed in creating harmony and balance within oneself. They believed that the best way to create this balance between our bodily humors was to drain whatever was in excess; an oozing wound would be treated by draining the pus and bile, a high fever would be treated by leeching the body to drain it of the bad blood.

If we jump ahead in time to Europe in the medieval era, say around 1830, bloodletting was immensely popular and a lucrative business. Leeches were used to treat almost any ailment; they kind of were like the aspirin of the past. France alone used to import 40 million leeches each year—that's a lot of squiggly, black worms in barrels.

When doctors became more sane and rational, and modern technology prevailed over crazy ancient healing methods, bloodletting died out. However, scientists have recently discovered that they might have been too quick to pass a judgment on leeches.

Leeches have now made their way back into hospital wards, with many doctors endorsing their use as a safe and effective way to drain blood after microsurgery. Big hospitals, such as the UCLH in London, are notorious for using these bloodthirsty grubs to suck out all the excess blood from their patients after microsurgery; they claim it's less painful than using needles, and leeches promote the body's natural healing abilities.

Leeches are also being used by modern doctors to help in postoperative care for skin grafts for burn victims, draining excess blood after somebody loses a finger, or reattaching lost fingers or ears. This is because leeches naturally produce a protein that prevents blood from clotting. This actually gives our tiny veins time to heal, by knitting themselves back together.

Leeching is now considered to be so beneficial, that Wales has become the new center for leech therapy. It hosts a farm responsible for supplying tens of thousands of medicinal leeches, which are purchased by hospitals around the world. How about that? Would you ever consent to being leeched? Think about it!

Willow

Willow has been a sacred plant in indigenous culture. Beyond that, willow has always been significant to ancient races; the ancient Egyptians swore by using the bark of a willow tree as a pain relief medicine, and so did Hippocrates. When it was scientifically tested by the Royal Society in 1763, they proved this belief and made it a scientific fact. However, it was not until 1915 that pharmaceutical titan Bayer used the active ingredient in willow bark to produce aspirin and sold it over the counter.

Scientists are still studying all the medicinal properties of the willow tree, and it is now a subject of almost a thousand scientific studies every year. They have discovered that the willow bark is much more than just a painkiller. It can also reduce the risk of strokes and even help prevent cancer. Is there anything miraculous that aspirin can't do? Little wonder we pop it for almost any aches and pains!

Snowdrops

Despite the dainty name, this herb packs a powerful punch. Snowdrops contain Galantamine, a substance that is now being used to treat Alzheimer's disease.

Even though the Soviet Union was the first country to begin investigating it and its properties, folklore speaks of ancient Bulgarians rubbing snowdrop flowers on their foreheads to cure migraine headaches. They have been an integral part of traditional medicine, much before the Soviet's started to officially look into the herb and its uses. Many ancient people in Europe used to grow snowdrops in their gardens, and used it to treat diseases and afflictions related to memory and headache.

Cow Stomach Juice

Wait, what? Yes, you read correctly. The juice from a cow's stomach has long been believed to have healing properties. In fact, an old recipe for an 'eye-salve' was found in a thousand year old Anglo-Saxon medical textbook. The book was called *Bald's Leechbook*, and it included a recipe that indicated the use of cow's stomach juice, also known as stomach bile from a cow, combined with garlic, onions, and wine. The instructions were to crush these ingredients together and leave them marinating in a bronze vessel for nine days and nights. This was considered to be a very potent and effective eye-salve, popular in medieval times.

Modern science has now discovered that despite the ick factor, ye olden doctors weren't absolutely crazy. Tests have been conducted on the eye-salve, showing that it kills MRSA bacteria in the lab faster than the best antibiotic available to modern medicine. Even though Anglo-Saxon remedies have a reputation for being disgusting and barbaric, that doesn't mean some of them are not effective. We are pretty judgmental these days; we think because we have technology, we are the smartest race, and the fact that ancient medicine is married so closely with superstition, often ends up leaving us underestimating the wisdom behind it. Old remedies do work; we need to let go of our rigid beliefs and give them a shot so we might actually learn something and benefit from the knowledge that our predecessors had learned through such difficult times and in such difficult odds.

Chapter 3: Encyclopedia of Herbs

With modern medicine being on the rise and extensive research conducted on the side effects of modern medicine, the interest in revival of herbal medicine and medicinal botanicals has been growing rapidly. Both the physicians and the patients are showing keen interest in and opting for alternative medicine and healing owing to the less detrimental and magical healing properties of herbs.

Even though there has not been sufficient scientific research to fully back the use of these herbs for healing, more modern consumers are choosing to vest their faith in these herbs, believing the rich lore associated with them.

Modern markets have seen a rise in the demand, and consequently manufacturing of herbal dietary supplements for enhanced health and healing. Yet the herbs sold in the open market are only a fraction of what we believe was known to the indigenous inhabitants of the North American continent.

Here we are going to review some of the herbs known and used by native people of North America, the compounds present in them responsible for their healing power, and the process by which they yield these benefits. Interestingly, the indigenous people used a combination of these herbs, some as medicine and the rest as staples of their Native American diet.

Additionally, Native American healers consider food itself to be a medicine. Furthermore, the process of procuring these herbs and preparing the food was believed to be a form of prayer. Thus, an element of respect and sacredness was attached to most of the plant and herbs.

It is interesting to note that even though some of these herbs are used across the world in modern cuisine and even in modern American foods, their spiritual relevance and connection to the native culture has been largely forgotten.

For example garlic, a staple modern spice, was known to and used by North American Indians (Cherokee people) for its diuretic and stimulant properties. Garlic tonic was used to treat cathartic syndrome, scurvy, severe asthma, and prevention of worms. Nowadays, garlic can be found in just every kitchen, but sadly it is only used for its aroma or distinct taste.

Keen attention was paid to the process of collecting and preserving these herbs and plants, much of which is lost now. It was believed that such attention to detail increased the efficacy and preserved the sanctity of the plant. For example, Native American Herbalists would consider the season, the time of year, and even the hour of day while collecting samples. Additionally, prayers were said and offerings were made which were believed to enhance the healing ability of the plant. The herbalist would then carefully select the part (roots, stem, leaves or the fruit/ seed) of the plant.

Following is a list of the most popular herbs and plants and their uses as known to the Native Americans.

1. **Ginseng (*Panax quinquefolius*)**

This plant is native to the deciduous forests found in the Appalachian and Ozark region of North America. The root of this plant is extremely valuable as medicine. Only the most skilled spiritual leaders use it in medicine. This root can be used to treat digestive issues and to relieve pain. The Muscogee people use smashed root of ginseng to stop bleeding and brew it in tea to treat fevers and respiratory conditions. It is also used as an aphrodisiac by the Meskwaki tribe. The Cherokee, Creek, Fox, Delaware, Houma, Fox, and Iroquois tribes frequently used it in their remedies as well. It is commonly used to treat stress, asthma, rheumatism, fevers, tuberculosis, and as a strengthener. Ginseng has been used for hundreds of years as a significant herb in traditional Chinese medicine. They believe it prolongs life, cures impotence and treats diabetes, fatigue, and cancer as well. Asian Ginseng has a warm and drying effect whereas American Ginseng is considered moist and cool in comparison. This herb is generally used to treat heatstroke and dryness in the body and is extra beneficial in treating chronic dry cough.

2. Coneflower (*Echinacea*)

This herb is also known as the purple coneflower. It has been an important ingredient for herbal medicine for centuries, used by the indigenous people of Choctaw, Cheyenne, Dokota, Kiowa, Omaha Pawnee, Sioux, Winnebago, and Montana. The coneflower is often used for pain relief and to treat illnesses such as mumps, smallpox, measles, arthritis, and rheumatism. It is also used in antidotes for most poisons and venoms.

3. Meadow Garlic (*Allium canadense*)

A species of garlic found mostly in eastern North America from Texas to Florida to New Brunswick to Montana. Long before antibiotics were invented, Native Americans used the garlic bulb as nature's antibiotic. The sulfur's glycosides in the garlic are responsible for its distinct smell and antibiotic properties. **Indigenous healers recommended garlic to people suffering from depression because it has a stimulating effect.** American Indians (Cherokee people) used garlic for its diuretic and stimulant properties. Garlic tonic was used to treat cathartic, scurvy, severe asthma, and to prevent worms.

4. Goldenseal (*Hydrastis canadensis*)

Also known as orangeroot or yellow puccoon, this herb is grown perennially in the eastern United States. It has enjoyed long standing popularity amongst certain Native American tribes of North America; they use it as both medicine and as a coloring material. It was used by Cherokee, Iroquois, and Micmac as treatment for fever, cough, pneumonia, upper respiratory tract infections, as well as to treat a stuffy nose and hay fever. It was also used for controlling internal bleeding and bleeding after childbirth.

5. St John's Wort (*Hypericumperforatum*)

A sprawling, leafy herb that grows in temperate areas. It was traditionally believed to ward off evil on St. John's feast and hence got its name. It has been used by Cherokee, Iroquois, and Montagnais to treat fever, coughs, sores, and abrasions, especially those involving nerve damage, bowel complaints, anxiety, depression, cuts, and burns. This herb can be harmful for livestock to ingest and can react adversely with prescription drugs.

6. Evening Primrose (*Oenothera biennis*)

This herb is native to eastern and central America. It was originally used as a poultice to hasten the wound healing process.
It was also used as an infusion for its astringent and sedative properties.
The Cherokee used this herb by heating and applying the root to hemorrhoids, while the Iroquois used it as a salve to treat skin issues. Ojibwa and Potawatomi used to relieve premenstrual and menstrual pain and to treat obesity and bowel pain.

7. Cranberry (*Vaccinium macrocarpon*)

Also called bitter berries, they can be found along the northern portion of the United States from Maine to Wisconsin, and along the Appalachians to North Carolina. Cranberries were traditionally used by the Montagnais as medicine to treat arrow wounds. They also used it to dye their rugs and blankets. One the most popular uses of cranberry include using it as pemmican, a high-protein combination of crushed cranberries, dried deer meat, and melted fat. Pilgrims and other early settlers ate the berries to fight off scurvy. It is also good for treating bladder and kidney problems.

8. Yarrow (*Achillea millefolium*)

This aromatic herb is widely found in the temperate regions of North America. Native Americans and early settlers used yarrow for its astringent qualities. Yarrow is beneficial for providing pain relief, it helps heal wounds and stop bleeding. The Navajo considered Yarrow to be a "life medicine;" they chewed on the plant to treat toothaches and used its infusions to relieve earaches. The Miwok used the plant as an analgesic and as a head cold remedy. The Cherokee drink a tea made from common yarrow to reduce fevers and bring about a restful sleep. The Zuni people use juice from the Yarrow plant to soothe burns whereas Ojibwe people smoke yarrow to alleviate headaches and stomach ailments.

9. Common Nettle (*Urticadioica*)

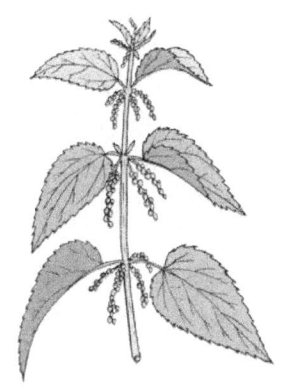

Also known as stinging nettle, it is abundantly found in areas where it rains a lot every year. It has traditionally been used for various treatments, such as for joint pain, anemia, eczema, arthritis, gout, and treatment of scalp seborrhea.

10. Tansy (*Tanacetum vulgare*)

Grown in northern parts of America, Tansy has been used for treating digestive tract problems. These include stomach and intestinal ulcers, certain gallbladder conditions, gas, bloating, stomachache, stomach spasms, and poor appetite. Its healing powers enable it to treat intestinal worms, epileptic seizures, hysteria, and tuberculosis.

11. Witch Hazel (*Hamamelis virginiana*):

This plant is most commonly found in eastern North America. Native American herbalists steep shrubs and stems of this plant to prepare a concoction which was used to treat swelling, inflammations, and tumors. The barks and leaves were used to treat external wounds, inflammation, rash, and as a popular disinfectant.

12. **Bloodroot (*Sanguinaria canadensis*)**

A flowering plant native to eastern Asia and Eastern North America, it has been used by Native Americans for its curative properties. It has been found effective in treatments of pneumonia, coughs, weak lungs, asthma, kidney, liver, bladder, or any stomach troubles, and as a great blood and nerve tonic.

Even though most of these plants are readily available in our farmer's market or super stores and some even locally grown in our gardens, there is little to no scientific data available on the effectiveness of them being used, and more importantly, methods for being used as home remedies. Additionally, there are a multitude of ways in which these plants and herbs were incorporated and ingested by the Native American tribes, with each tribe having their own preferred species and method owing to their diverse culture and distinct location. However, much of this knowledge is lost considering it was scarcely documented and almost always handed down orally from one generation to another.

It is for these reasons there is a wide disparity in the processes and methodologies of formulating saps and tonics. Another interesting fact, which adds further complexity, is the influence and impact of the travelers. Settlers from other parts of the world brought to the American indigenous people their own variety of herbs, it may sometimes only be a different species of the same herb but with radically different chemical composition. Hence, it is imperative to acknowledge that unlike modern medicine, regardless of the precession, uniformity in terms of consistency and effectiveness can never be guaranteed with botanical medicines.

Furthermore, each individual plant or herb is a composite of multiple compounds. Not all of these compounds are effective in treating a specific problem at hand and where one compound in the herb may be beneficial for treating a disease, another compound in the same herb might be detrimental. Hence caution must be taken to prevent herbal toxicity and drug interaction. Isolating a chemical compound from a herb is a rather difficult intricacy, tools for which were not available to Native Americans. They based their judgment on the effect of an herb in alleviating pain and the symptoms. There remains room for clinical trials and detailed scientific research in this regard.

Following are some ways in which the above listed herbs were consumed by the Native

American tribes.

1. **Cold water extract of herbs:** This process is used to avoid oxidation of the compounds present in herbs as very high temperatures tend to modify or destroy some important chemical compounds present in the herbs. Maceration is one form of cold water extraction where the plant is cut into small pieces and immersed in a liquid (water, oil, alcohol) at room temperature. The process works by softening and eventually breaking the plant skin. Maceration of a plant in water or alcohol will yield a tincture, whereas glyceryl macerates use a mixture of alcohol and glycerin.

2. **Filtrates for herbal tonics:** Percolation is a process in which the solvent (water, oil, alcohol, glycerin, etc.) is made to move through a powdered herb very slowly. The solvent is then passed through a filter and collected in a container. The solvent thus collected has herbal essence and constituents. This method is considered, by herbalists, to yield a 30% stronger product.

3. **Infusion of leaves and roots:** Infusion is a similar process in which the plant is allowed to steep in the liquid (oil mostly) for a prolonged period of time. Maceration is different from infusion in that during maceration the essence of the liquid is added to the plant or herb, whereas during infusion, the extract of the plant is added to the liquid.

4. **Grounded and smashed:** Seed, grains, roots, and dried hard herbs are grinded using a grinding stone. Some herbs are air or sun dried before grinding. This process is used for making herbal powders which can be used and stored for a very long time.

5. **Juicing:** The process of extracting the sap of a plant by applying pressure or grinding. It removes the solid matter including the skin, seeds, and pulp yielding a liquid that contains most of the minerals and chemicals found in the plant.

6. **Topical application:** A variety of herbal medicines have been used traditionally for topical application to treat skin ailments, superficial cuts, and wounds. This has been a popular remedy as the harmful effects of botanical medicine are virtually non-existent. Most of the topically applied herbs are made into a thick paste; on occasions a band aid may be used to secure the applied position on the skin. Efficacy of the herb seems to depend largely on the plant used and the term of application.

7. **Herbal sweat baths**: One of the most used traditional methods by herbalists. There are many types of sweat baths for example, the pool or plunge sweat bath, water vapor or steam/smoke bath, and mixed type sweat bath. Different herbs or their extracts can be added to a natural or an artificial body of water and then immersing or bathing the patient. Heating may also be applied to the bath to achieve higher temperatures to enhance the aroma and effect of the herbs. The Native Americans of California have used steam and smoke baths for centuries. In such

baths, a much lesser quantity of water is used to prevent dilution of the herbs. The vapors or smoke is either inhaled or delivered to the affected area.

Although most of these herbs and methods are still being used, not only in America but all parts of the world, they are used with little knowledge of their efficacy or safety. Hence more attention and caution is needed while practicing any of these methods.

List of Medicinal Herbs and Their Properties

Herbs used medicinally can have many different properties and have actions that benefit the body in various ways. They can be helpful to our bodies, either as a whole, or they can have a single property that treats specific symptoms, or a single action that targets a specific malady afflicting our bodies.

Medicinal herbs must be used with caution, as they can have a direct impact on many different physical and psychological processes in our bodies. Before consuming any of these herbs, we need to carefully research how these properties affect different parts of the body and their impact on the disease or symptoms that we mean to treat.

We must also take care and learn about the different attributes of each plant in order to figure out which herb is the best to use as treatment for any illness or disease.

The following is a list of medicinal herbs and their properties so that you can explore each herb according to its function and use it in accordance. They are mentioned alphabetically so you can refer to this list as a glossary of herbs as well.

A

Abortifacient

These are herbs that can induce abortion. They must not be taken without proper medical advice from an expert. These were used in ancient traditions to induce abortion, as they contain strong astringents or have powerful stimulating properties. The stimulating properties in these herbs can cause the muscles in the uterus to contract, inducing abortion.

The following herbs have abortifacient properties and have been used since ancient times for this purpose only:

- Common Rue (Ruta Graveolens)
- Tansy (Tanacetum Vulgare)
- Parsley (Petroselinum Crispum)
- Southernwood (Artemisia Abrotanum)
- Male Fern (Dryopteris Filix-Mas)
- Bog Myrtle (Myrica Gale)
- Juniper (Juniperus Communis)
- Yarrow (Achillea Millefolium)
- Wormseed (Chenopodium Ambrosioides)
- Blue Cohosh (Caulophyllum Thalictroides)

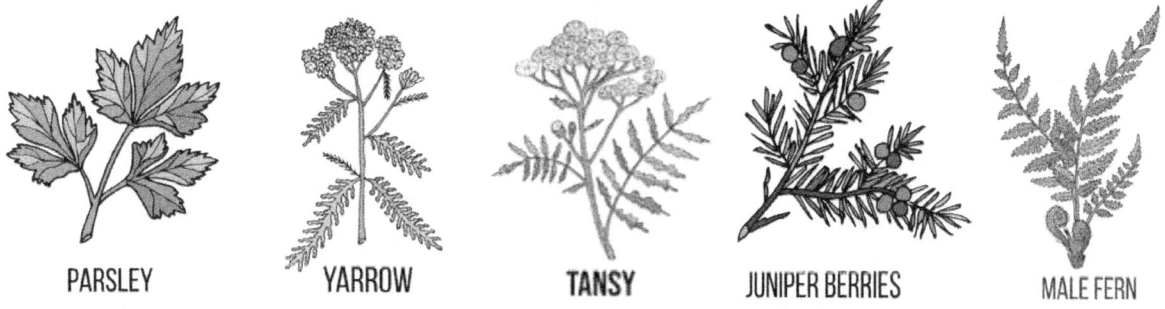

PARSLEY   YARROW   TANSY   JUNIPER BERRIES   MALE FERN

Adaptogenic

These herbs are used to enhance our body's natural ability to deal with stressful situations of any sort. Since our bodies eventually adapt to stress, these herbs help expedite that process. This includes dealing with any kind of infections, mental or physical stress, environmental pressures and fatigue.

The following herbs have adaptogenic properties:

- Golden Root (Rhodiola Rosea)
- Schisandra (Schisandra Chinensis)
- Eleuthero (Eleutherococcus Senticosus)
- Ashwagandha (Withania Somnifera)
- Astragalus (Astragalus Membranaceus)
- Chaga Mushroom (Inonotus Obliquus)
- Reishi (Ganoderma Lucidum)

ASTRAGALUS

Alterative

These are herbs that slowly but gradually restore function in body parts that are sick and need to heal. They also stimulate our tissues and encourage white blood cell production in the body, speeding up healing processes and overall help increase our health and vitality.

The following herbs are considered to be alternatives:

- Purple Coneflower (Echinacea Purpurea)
- Red Clover (Trifolium Pratense)
- Blue Flag (Iris Versicolor)
- Burdock (Arctium Lappa)
- Sarsaparilla (Smilax Spp.)
- Cleavers (Galium Aparine)
- Stinging Nettle (Urtica Dioica)
- Yellow Dock (Rumex Crispus)
- Dandelion (Taraxacum Officinale)

CLEAVERS RED CLOVER SARSAPARILLA DANDELION BURDOCK

Analgesics

These herbs are accredited with having immense pain relieving qualities. They have played a vital role in healing since ancient times in many different civilizations around the world.

The following is a list of herbs with analgesic properties:

- Valerian (Valeriana Officinalis)
- California Poppy (Eschscholzia Californica)
- Kava Kava (Piper Methysticum)
- Passion Flower (Passiflora Incarnata)
- Arnica (Arnica Montana)—Only External Use
- Clove (Syzygium Aromaticum)
- Indian Pipe (Monotropa Uniflora)

CLOVE

Anaphrodisiac

These herbs have the exact opposite effect than aphrodisiacs; they diminish sexual appetite and kill the libido for a certain period. The effects are only temporary.

The following herbs are considered to be anaphrodisiacs:

- Chasteberry (Vitex Agnus-Castus)
- Hops (Humulus Lupulus)
- Common Rue (Ruta Graveolens)

COMMON RUE

Antacids

Antacid herbs are those which aid with digestion. They can neutralize extra acid produced in the stomach and intestines and help with stomach aches, indigestion and bloating.

The following herbs are considered to be antacids and are still used today as they were used centuries ago. They include:

- Comfrey (Symphytum Officinale)
- Flaxseed (Linum Usitatissimum)
- Meadowsweet (Filipendula Ulmaria)
- Dandelion Root (Taraxacum Officinale)
- Giant Kelp (Macrocystis Pyrifera)
- Great Mullein (Verbascum Thapsus)
- Red Raspberry (Rubus Idaeus)
- Slippery Elm (Ulmus Americana)
- Wood Betony (Stachys Officinalis)
- Bladderwrack (Fucus Vesiculosus)
- Irish Moss (Chondrus Crispus)

SLIPPERY ELM

DANDELION

FLAXSEED

COMFREY

Anthelmintic/Antiparasitic/Vermicide/Vermifuge

These are basically medicinal herbs that are used to kill intestinal worms or expel them from the digestive system. It is quite impressive that the Native Americans had this knowledge, but it makes sense as we consider how many foods they consume that are from the ground, organic, and natural.

The following herbs have anti-parasitic properties:

- Wormwood (Artemisia Absinthium)
- Tansy (Tanacetum Vulgare)
- Aloe (Aloe Vera)
- Garlic (Allium Sativum)
- Thuja (Thuja Occidentalis)
- Mountain Flax (Linum Catharticum)

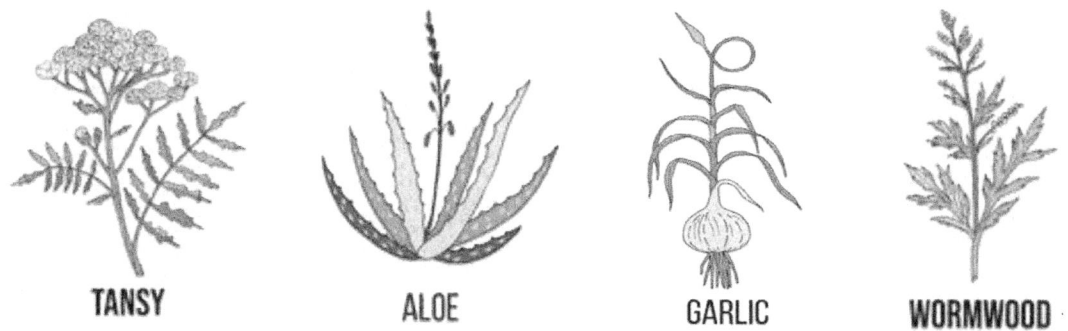

TANSY   ALOE   GARLIC   WORMWOOD

Anti-Abortive

The opposite of abortifacient herbs, these herbs actually help reduce abortive tendencies. These herbs are taken in miniscule quantities in the early stages of pregnancies, believing that this would help the mother carry the baby to term without fear of miscarriage. However, if the fetus is already damaged or not properly secured, these herbs would not work.

Here are a few examples of anti-abortive herbs:

- Cramp Bark (Viburnum Opulus)
- Raspberry Leaf (Rubus Idaeus)
- American Mistletoe (Phoradendron Leucarpum)
- Pennyroyal (Mentha Pulegium)
- Ragwort (Senecio Jacobaea)

PENNYROYAL

Antiallergic

These herbs are taken when a person is suffering from an allergic reaction. They help reduce the intensity of allergic reaction and can also work as a supportive therapy for a person with allergies, as it promotes the body's natural ability to produce antihistamines by stabilizing our mast cells.

The following herbs have anti-allergic properties:

- Stinging Nettle (Urtica Dioica)
- Chinese Skullcap (Scutellaria Baicalensis)
- Chamomile (Matricaria Recutita)
- Feverfew (Tanacetum Parthenium)

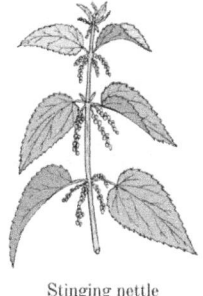

Stinging nettle

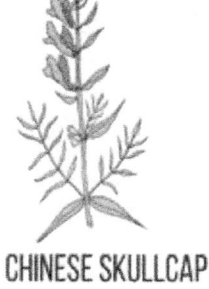

CHINESE SKULLCAP

CHAMOMILE

Antiasthmatic

These are herbs that help alleviate symptoms of asthma. Some of these herbs carry strong antispasmodic properties. These help dilate the bronchioles while some herbs help dissolve mucus. These herbs can also be smoked as they act fastest that way, bringing quick relief.

Some examples of anti-asthmatic herbs include:

- Coltsfoot (Tussilago Farfara)
- Great Mullein (Verbascum Thapsus)
- Lobelia (Lobelia Inflata)
- Wild Cherry Bark (Prunus Virginiana)
- Yerba Santa (Eriodictyon Californicum)
- Dwarf Mallow (Malva Neglecta)

LOBELIA

Antibilious

These are purely medicinal herbs that help stimulate the production and flow of bile from the liver. Herbs with anti-bilious properties include:

- Balmony (Chelone Glabra)
- Fringetree (Chionanthus Virginica)
- Barberry (Berberis Vulgaris)
- GoldenSeal (Hydrastis Canadensis)

GOLDENSEAL

Antibacterial/Antibiotic/Bactericidal

These are herbs that prevent the growth of bacteria in the body, eliminate any bacteria that are already present inside, and it stimulates the immune system as well. These herbs play a vital part in healing, as a lot of modern medicine relies on these herbs for their antibiotic properties.

These are some herbs that can be considered as antibacterial or antibiotic:

- Thyme (Thymus Vulgaris)
- Barberry (Berberis Vulgaris)
- GoldenSeal (Hydrastis Canadensis)
- Echinacea (Echinacea Purpurea)
- Garlic (Allium Sativum)
- Old Man's Beard (Usnea Spp.)
- Lemon Balm (Melissa Officinalis)
- Common Plantain (Plantago Major)
- Chaparral (Larrea Tridentata)

THYME   GOLDENSEAL   GARLIC   LEMON BALM

Anticatarrhal

Anticatarrhal herbs are those that prevent or remove extra mucus produced by the body, especially from the sinuses. It basically prevents excessive mucus production from the upper respiratory tract. Here are a few herbs that can perform this function:

- Pepper (Piper Nigrum)
- Cayenne Pepper (Capsicum Annuum/Capisicum Frutescens)
- Ginger (Zingiber Officinale)
- Garlic (Allium Sativum)
- Sage (Salvia Officinalis)
- Cinnamon (Cinnamomum Verum)
- Anise (Pimpinella Anisum)
- Goldenrod (Solidago Virgaurea)
- Great Mullein (Verbascum Thapsus)
- Eyebright (Euphrasia Officinalis)
- Comfrey (Symphytum Officinale)
- Bistort (Persicaria Bistorta)
- Horseradish (Cochlearia Armoracia)
- Houndstongue (Cynoglossum Officinale)

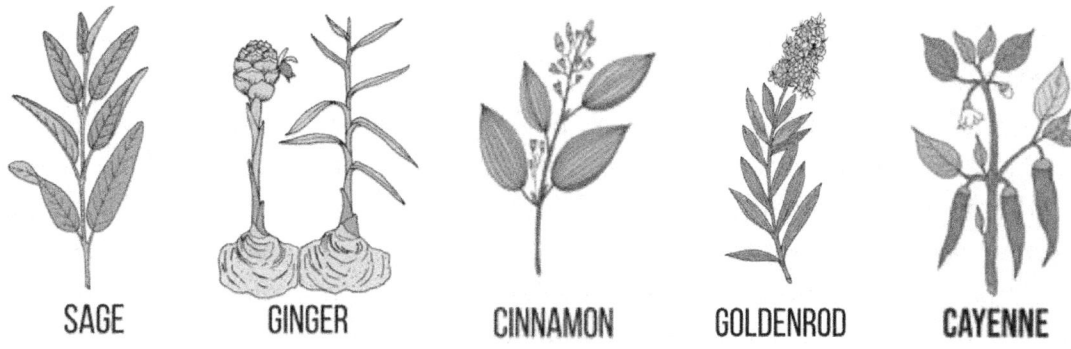

SAGE GINGER CINNAMON GOLDENROD CAYENNE

Anticoagulant

Anticoagulant herbs have the ability to prevent and dissolve blood clots. These herbs must not be used casually, especially in combination with allopathic anticoagulants, which people normally take after surgery as well.

The following plants have anticoagulant properties:

- Garlic (Allium Sativum)
- Ginger (Zingiber Officinale)
- Bilberry (Vaccinium Myrtillus)
- Bladderwrack (Fucus Vesiculosus)
- Laminaria (Laminaria Digitata)
- Yellow Sweet Clover (Melilotus Officinalis)
- White Sweet Clover (Melilotus Albus)

BILBERRY

Anticonvulsant/Antiepileptic

These are herbs that are used to treat patients suffering from epilepsy or seizures. The usage of these herbs can successfully reduce or prevent seizures in patients. Here are a few examples of anticonvulsant herbs used by Native Americans to prevent seizures caused by epilepsy and other reasons:

- Black Cohosh (Actaea Racemosa)
- Indian Pipe (Monotropa Uniflora)
- Kava Kava (Piper Methysticum)
- Valerian (Valeriana Officinalis)

BLACK COHOSH   **KAVA**

Antidepressant

Did you know that many antidepressants can be found in nature? There are several herbs that help relieve the symptoms of depression and can really act as useful tools to provide supportive therapy for people who suffer from mild to moderate depression. They are also a good option for people who want to treat symptoms of depression without taking synthetic antidepressants that have unpleasant side-effects such as weight gain and drowsiness. Antidepressant herbs are also considered adaptogens at times.

Here are some herbs that have antidepressant qualities:

- St. John's Wort (Hypericum Perforatum)
- Lavender (Lavandula Angustifolia)
- Golden Root (Rhodiola Rosea)
- Schisandra (Schisandra Chinensis)
- Passion Flower (Passiflora Incarnata)

ST JOHNS WORT   **LAVENDER**

Antidiarrheal

Antidiarrheal herbs are a great option for people who suffer from an upset stomach and loose movements but synthetic medicine does not suit them. These herbs help treat and prevent diarrhea as they have high tannin content.

Here are some examples of herbs that help prevent diarrhea:

- Tormentil Potentilla Erecta)
- Silverweed (Potentilla Anserina)
- Raspberry (Rubus Idaeus)
- Houndstongue (Cynoglossum Officinale)
- Staghorn Sumac (Rhus Typhina)
- Wild Strawberry (Fragaria Vesca)
- Psyllium Seed (Plantago Afra)
- Dogwood (Cornus Florida)

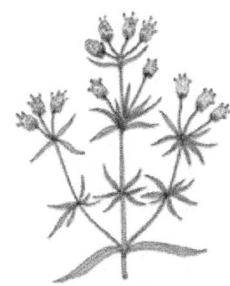

PSYLLIUM

Antiemetic

Antiemetic herbs are excellent for people who feel nauseous and are about to vomit. Active agents in these herbs help reduce feelings of nausea and prevent vomiting.

Here are some examples of antiemetic herbs:

- Ginger (Zingiber Officinale)
- Dill (Anethum Graveolens)
- Black Horehound (Ballota Nigra)
- Fennel (Foeniculum Vulgare)
- Spearmint (Mentha Spicata Lemon)
- Lemon Balm (Melissa Officinalis)
- Peppermint (Mentha X Piperita)

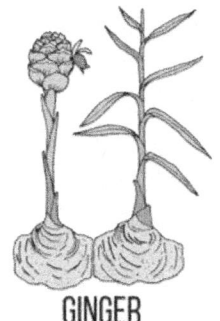   

GINGER   **FENNEL SEED**   **LEMON BALM**   **PEPPERMINT**

53

Anti-inflammatory

Even though there are a lot of synthetic anti-inflammatory medicines available over the counter, people still prefer to take a more natural approach because they consider it to be a safer option with fewer side effects. There are many herbs that naturally have anti-inflammatory properties. Different herbs have different ways of working, but they rarely ever are used to directly treat a symptom. They work indirectly, by boosting the body's natural anti-inflammatory processes to facilitate healing.

Here are some medicinal herbs that have anti-inflammatory properties:

- Meadowsweet (Filipendula Ulmaria)
- Witch Hazel (Hamamelis Virginiana)
- Yarrow (Achillea Millefolium)
- Marigold Flowers (Calendula Officinalis)
- Sheep Sorrel (Rumex Acetosella)
- Turmeric (Curcuma Longa)
- Solomon's seal (Polygonatum Biflorum)

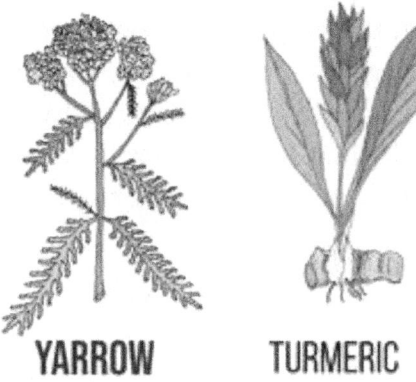

YARROW   **TURMERIC**

Antilithic/Lithotriptic

These are herbs that are used to remove kidney stones and gallstones and are also used to prevent them from forming. Even though most people rely on western medicine to treat these symptoms, herbal treatments are known to be effective and can expedite the process of expelling these stones from the body.

Here are some examples of herbs that help prevent and treat kidney stones and gallstones that form in our bodies:

Sassafras

- Maize (Zea Mays)
- Hydrangea (Hydrangea Arborescens)
- Pipsissewa (Chimaphila Umbellata)
- Sassafras (Sassafras Albidum)
- Bearberry (Arctostaphylos Uva-Ursi)
- Common Groundsel (Senecio Vulgaris)

Antioxidant

Antioxidants are amazing for detoxifying the body and reducing the amount of free radicals that form within. Many natural fruits and herbs contain antioxidants and these help prevent damage to our cells.

Here are some herbs that naturally contain antioxidants:

- Ashwagandha (Withania Somnifera)
- Astragalus (Astragalus Membranaceus)
- Bacopa (Bacopa Monnieri)
- Green Tea (Camellia Sinensis)
- Autumn Olive (Elaeagnus Umbellata)
- Lemon Balm (Melissa Officinalis)
- Turmeric (Curcuma Longa)

ASHWAGHANDA   ASTRAGALUS   BACOPA   GREEN TEA   LEMON BALM   TURMERIC

Antiprostatic

Antiprostatic herbs are plants that naturally alleviate symptoms caused by an enlarged prostate. Prostate health is very important and naturally being able to treat these symptoms helps avoid side effects that come with synthetic medicine.

Here are some herbs that reduce symptoms caused by an enlarged prostate:

- **Saw Palmetto** (Serenoa Repens)
- Small Flowered Willow Herb (Epilobium Parviflorum)
- Stinging Nettle (Urtica Dioica)

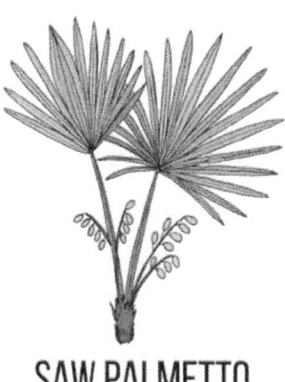

SAW PALMETTO

Antipruritic

There are some medicinal herbs that carry antipruritic properties. This means that they can be used to prevent or relieve itching. These herbs are helpful when suffering from rashes or dry, flaky, irritated skin. They can be applied topically in the form of an ointment or consumed.

Here are some medicinal herbs that help soothe irritated and itchy skin:

- Butcher's Broom (Ruscus Aculeatus)
- Chickweed (Stellaria Media)
- Kudzu (Pueraria Lobata)
- Scarlet Pimpernel (Anagallis Arvensis)
- Vervain (Verbena Officinalis)

BUTCHERS BROOM

Antipyretic/Febrifuge

Native Americans used these herbs to help bring down fever and to avoid getting high fevers to begin with. These herbs have been used by people throughout history to treat fevers.

Here are some examples of herbs that can be used to treat fever:

- White Willow Bark (Salix Alba)
- Bunchberry (Cornus Canadensis)
- Skullcap (Scutellaria Lateriflora)
- Elderberry (Sambucus Nigra)
- Dulse (Palmaria Palmata)
- Peruvian Bark (Cinchona Succirubra)
- Lady's Mantle (Alchemilla Vulgaris)
- Southernwood (Artemisia Abrotanum)
- Bloodroot (Sanguinaria Canadensis)

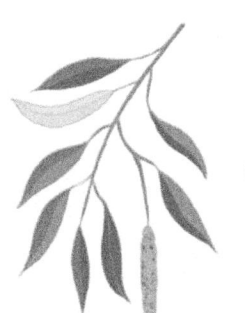
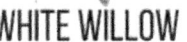

WHITE WILLOW   **ELDERBERRY**

Antiretroviral

These are herbs that are used effectively alongside modern medication to treat retroviruses. They either alleviate the intensity of the symptoms or provide relief from pain. Retroviruses include RNA viruses such as HIV. While these herbs don't treat the viruses, they help manage them.

Here are a few examples of herbs that have anti-retroviral properties:

- Astragalus (Astragalus Membranaceus)
- Cat's Claw (Uncaria Tomentosa)
- Frost Grape (Vitis Vulpina)
- Shitake (Lentinula Edodes)
- Licorice (Glycyrrhiza Lepidota)

ASTRAGALUS   **CAT'S CLAW**   **LICORICE**

Antirheumatic

These are medicinal herbs that are used to relieve the painful symptoms of rheumatism, more commonly known as arthritis. Arthritis can cause debilitating pain in the bones and joints, and these herbs help provide pain relief and can also be taken to prevent arthritis as well. They can be used in the form of massage oils and creams to be applied topically, or in medication to be consumed internally, while some can be smoked to provide instant pain relief as well.

Here are some examples of anti-rheumatic herbs:

- Devil's Claw (Harpagophytum Procumbens)
- Stinging Nettle (Urtica Dioica)
- American Pokeweed (Phytolaca Americana)
- Celery Seed (Apium Graveolens)
- Sarsaparilla (Smilax Spp.)
- Wild Yam (Dioscorea Villosa)
- Cayenne (Capsicum Annuum)
- Curly Dock (Rumex Crispus)
- European Mistletoe (Viscum Album)
- Ginger (Zingiber Officinale)

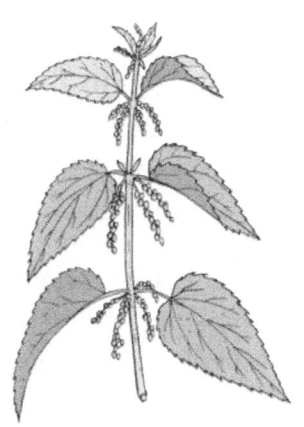

Stinging nettle

Antiseptic

There are many herbs that have natural antiseptic properties. These herbs slow down the growth of bacteria and prevent infection. Herbs with antiseptic properties are often crushed to release the action within. They are then used in ointments and other medication to help the healing process.

Here are a few herbs that naturally contain antiseptics:

- GoldenSeal (Hydrastis Canadensis)
- Nasturtium (Tropaeolum Majus)
- Barberry (Berberis Vulgaris)
- Black Walnut (Juglans Nigra)
- Sassafras (Sassafras Albidum)
- Iceland Moss (Cetraria Islandica)
- White Pond Lily (Nymphaea Odorata)
- Oregon Grape (Mahonia Aquifolium/Berberis Aquifolium)
- Bethroot (Trillium Erectum)

Sassafras

BARBERRY   **BLACK WALNUT**   **OREGON GRAPE ROOT**

Antispasmodic/Spasmolytic

These are medicinal herbs that help ease cramped and spasming muscles. They can also be used to prevent the muscles from seizing up and release tension that gets built up in them. They also help alleviate spasms, cramps, and tension in our nerves and organs as well.

There are certain antispasmodic herbs that act on specific organs or systems in our body, while others work on the body as a whole. These herbs are traditionally either applied topically in the form of ointments or unguents, or they can be taken internally as well.

Here are some examples of antispasmodic herbs:

- Valerian (Valeriana Officinalis)
- Great Mullein (Verbascum Thapsus)
- Virginia Springbeauty (Claytonia Virginica)
- Skullcap (Scutellaria Lateriflora)
- Lady's Slipper (Cypripedium Acaule)
- Indian Pipe (Monotropa Uniflora)
- Wild Yam (Dioscorea Villosa)
- Hops (Humulus Lupulus)
- Prickly Ash (Zanthoxylum Americanum)
- Lily Of The Valley (Convallaria Majalis)
- American Mistletoe (Phoradendron Leucarpum)
- Rosemary (Rosmarinus Officinalis)

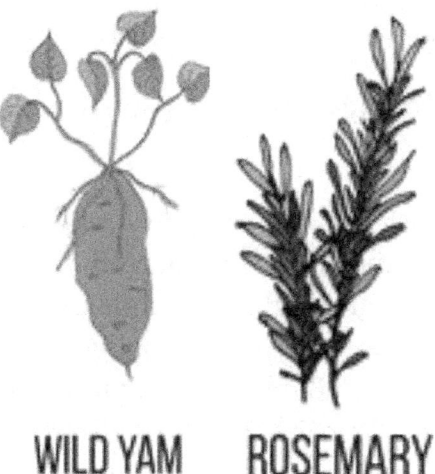

WILD YAM   ROSEMARY

Antitussive

Antitussive herbs are basically medicinal plants that help soothe a cough and reduce its severity. Native Americans made good use of these herbs to deal with the cold North American winters. These herbs can be taken internally as medicine or used in steam baths and inhaled as well.

Here are some medicinal herbs that carry antitussive properties:

- Licorice (Glycyrrhiza Glabra)
- Coltsfoot (Tussilago Farfara)
- Staghorn Sumac (Rhus Typhinaanise)
- Anise (Pimpinella Anisum)
- Houndstongue (Cynoglossum Officinale)
- Iceland Moss (Cetraria Islandica)
- Bunchberry (Cornus Canadensis)
- Opium (Poppy Tears, Lachryma Papaveris)

COLTSFOOT   LICORICE

Antiviral

Antiviral herbs have properties that inhibit or kill the growth of viruses. Some of these herbs also carry properties that boost our immune systems. They are effective to this day for people who are suffering from viral infections going around seasonally who do not want to take synthetic medicine, as it often contains properties that cause drowsiness. They are a great natural remedy and work effectively as well.

Here are some examples of medicinal antiviral herbs:

- Astragalus (Astragalus Membranaceus)
- Thuja (Thuja Occidentalis)
- Neem (Azadirachta Indica)
- St. John's Wort (Hypericum Perforatum)
- Lemon Balm (Melissa Officinalis)
- Greater Celandine (Chelidonium Majus)
- Yarrow (Achillea Millefolium)

ASTRAGALUS ST JOHNS WORT

Anxiolytic/Anti-anxiety/Anti-panic

It might surprise people to know that even hundreds of years ago, the indigenous people had ways of treating mental health. As the Native Americans gave a lot of importance to mental and spiritual health along with physical health, as they believed all of these elements are parts of the body that make it whole. So if any one element is lacking, the person is considered to be unwell.

Due to these beliefs, they had traditional remedies for anxiety relief that are meant to treat both the psychological symptoms and the physical symptoms that can arise because of it. People with anxiety suffer physical symptoms such as an upset stomach, shaky hands, shivering, migraine, and nausea along with several others.

Here are some medicinal herbs that are used to treat anxiety and panic disorders:

- Oat (Avena Sativa)
- California Poppy (Eschscholzia Californica)
- Kava-Kava (Piper Methysticum)
- Lavender (Lavandula Angustifolia)
- Valerian (Valeriana Officinalis)
- Passion Flower (Passiflora Incarnata)

LAVENDER

Aphrodisiac

Perhaps the most well-known category, aphrodisiacs are medicinal herbs that increase a person's sexual potency and desire. Different parts of a plant are considered to be aphrodisiacs and some foods as well. These can be ingested or smoked as well.

Here are some examples of herbs that are considered to be aphrodisiacs:

DAMIANA

- Golden Root (Rhodiola Rosea)
- Asian Ginseng (Panax Ginseng)
- Damiana (Turnera Diffusa)
- Rosemary (Rosmarinus Officinalis)
- Yerba Mate (Ilex Paraguariensis)
- American Ginseng (Panax Quinquefolius)
- Water Eryngo (Eryngium Aquaticum)

Aromatic

These are herbs that emit a strong, pleasant smell. They are used for aromatherapy in oils and as incense. Different scents are supposed to treat different symptoms such as anxiety, tiredness, stress, insomnia, and depression, along with many others. The aromatic oils are sometimes massaged into the skin, or the herbs are burned in the form of incense to let out a soothing aroma.

Aromatic herbs are also used in cooking, to enhance the flavor and the appetite, and to add taste to herbal mixtures as well.

Here are some herbs that are used for aromatherapy and cooking:

- Anise (Pimpinella Anisum)
- Caraway (Carum Carvi)
- Allspice (Pimenta Dioica)
- Dill (Anethum Graveolens)
- Fennel (Foeniculum Vulgare)
- Cubeb (Piper Cubeba)
- True Cardamom (Elettaria Cardamomum)
- True Cinnamon Tree (Cinnamomum Verum)
- Clove (Syzygium Aromaticum)
- Coriander (Coriandrum Sativum)
- Ginger (Zingiber Officinale)

- Peppermint (Mentha X Piperita)
- Orris Root (Iris Germanica).
- Lavender (Lavandula × Intermedia)

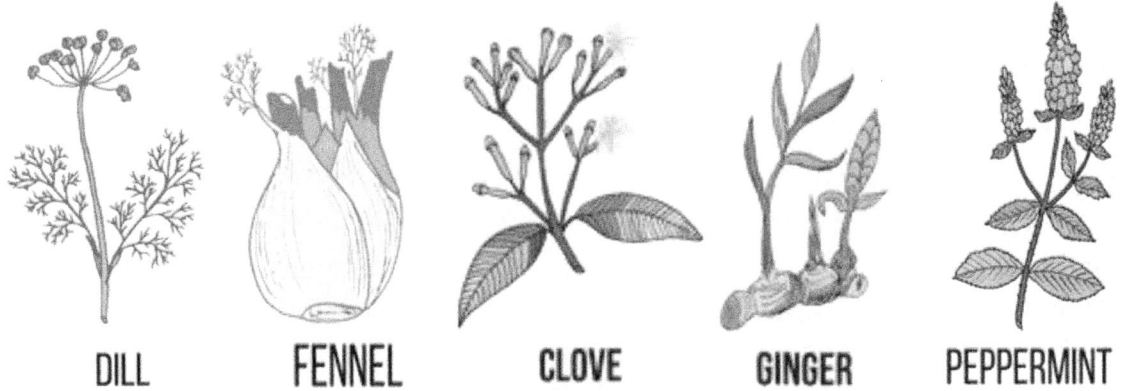

DILL   FENNEL   CLOVE   GINGER   PEPPERMINT

Astringent

Astringents are basically medicinal herbs that act in a binding or constricting way on our mucous membranes, skin, and other tissues. The purpose of these herbs is to restrict the amount of mucus being discharged from our bodies and also to stem the flow of blood. These herbs are frequently used to treat painful ailments such as hemorrhoids and diarrhea.

Herbs are considered to be astringent if they are rich in tannins. Tannins are basically substances that are found in vast amounts in the bark of specific trees and they contain agents that bind the flow of mucus and blood.

Here are some medicinal astringent herbs:

- Witch Hazel (Hamamelis Virginiana)
- Horse Chestnut (Aesculus Hippocastanum)
- Common Oak (Quercus Spp.)
- Shepherd's Purse (Capsella Bursa-Pastoris)
- Horsetail (Equisetum Arvense)
- Agrimony (Agrimonia Eupatoria)
- Tormentil (Potentilla Erecta)
- Silverweed (Potentilla Anserina)
- Knotweed (Polygonum Aviculare)
- Rhatany (Krameria Lappacea)
- Common Plantain (Plantago Major)
- Greater Periwinkle (Vinca Major)

AGRIMONY

62

B

Bitter/Bitter tonic/Stomachic

These are herbs that although taste bitter, have properties that stimulate the production of hormones in our digestive system, increasing the appetite as a result. These herbs have been used for centuries by indigenous people as well as people in the medieval times to help cure stomach ailments and increase hunger, as it was believed strong bodies are well-fed. 'Bitters' still serve as digestive aids in some parts of the world.

Here are a few examples of herbal bitters:

- Bogbean (Menyanthes Trifoliata)
- Gentian (Gentiana Lutea/Gentiana Acaulis/ Gentiana Scabra)
- Centaury (Centaurium Erythraea)
- Wormwood (Artemisia Absinthium)
- Yarrow (Achillea Millefolium)
- Dandelion (Taraxacum Officinale)
- Hops (Humulus Lupulus)
- Artichoke (Cynara Scolymus)

CENTAURY   WORMWOOD   YARROW   DANDELION

Bronchospasmolytic

These herbs are used to suppress spasms in the lower airways of our windpipe and lungs. They are used to treat sudden spasms to provide relief to the sufferer. These herbs can be inhaled in the form of steam or ingested.

Here are some examples of herbs that can suppress spasms felt in the lower airways:

- Coleus(Coleus Forskohlii)
- Elecampane (Inula Helenium)
- Grindelia (Grindelia Camporum / Grindelia Robusta)

C

Cardioprotective

Cardio-protective herbs function by protecting the muscle tissue in our hearts from lack of oxygen. This helps lessen the risk of heart damage by a considerable degree. Agents from these herbs are used in modern medicine to this day.

Here are a few examples of cardio-protective medicinal herbs:

- Hawthorn (Crataegus Monogyna/Crataegus Laevigata)
- Asian Ginseng (Panax Ginseng)

Carminative

Carminative herbs help reduce stomach ache by enabling the stomach and intestinal wall to relax. This releases intestinal gas and alleviates any symptoms of stomach ache and discomfort. These herbs usually have a high content of essential oils and are very effective at treating gastrointestinal pain.

Here are some examples of medicinal herbs that carry carminative properties:

- Anise (Pimpinella Anisum)
- Caraway (Carum Carvi)
- Dill (Anethum Graveolens)
- Fennel (Foeniculum Vulgare)
- Ginger (Zingiber Officinale)
- Turmeric (Curcuma Longa)
- Lemon Balm (Melissa Officinalis)
- Wintergreen (Gaultheria Procumbens)
- Rosemary (Rosmarinus Officinalis)
- Peppermint (Mentha X Piperita)
- Bergamot (Citrus Bergamia)
- Chickweed (Stellaria Media)

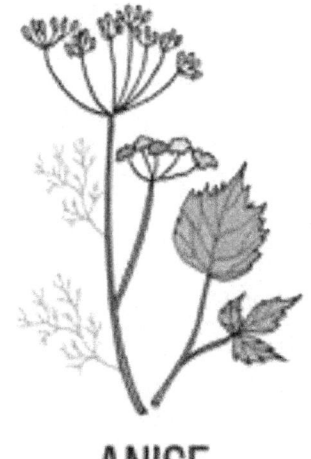

ANISE

Choleretic/Cholagogue

These are herbs that stimulate the production of bile in the liver. This is helpful, as bile helps break down fats in our small intestine. Insufficient production of bile and blockages in the flow of the bile can cause gallstones, cirrhosis and even cancer.

Here are some herbs that help increase the production of bile in our liver:

- Dandelion (Taraxacum Officinale)
- Milk Thistle (Silybum Marianum)
- Greater Bindweed (Convolvulus Sepium)
- Artichoke (Cynara Scolymus)
- GoldenSeal (Hydrastis Canadensis)
- Greater Celandine (Chelidonium Majus)
- Turmeric (Curcuma Longa)
- Hemp Agrimony (Eupatorium Cannabinum)
- Soapwort (Saponaria Officinalis)

DANDELION   MILK THISTLE   GOLDENSEAL   CELANDINE   TURMERIC

Circulatory Stimulant

These are medicinal herbs that increase the blood flow in our body, stimulating blood flow from the heart to different tissues and organs in our body.

Here are a few examples of herbal circulatory stimulants:

- Ginkgo (Ginkgo Biloba)
- Hawthorn (Crataegus Monogyna/Crataegus Laevigata)
- Ginger (Zingiber Officinale)
- Rosemary (Rosmarinus Officinalis)

GINKGO BILOBA

Contraceptive

These are medicinal herbs that have been used to prevent pregnancy for centuries. They have not always been the most effective, because getting the correct brew was a difficult task in the olden days. These herbs used to be brewed as a tea, called 'moon-tea', and drank by women to prevent pregnancy. If the tea was brewed correctly and consumed at the right time, it did in fact, prevent pregnancy.

Here are some examples of herbal contraceptives:

- Virginia Spring Beauty (Claytonia Virginica)
- Queen Anne's Lace (Wild Carrot)
- Blue Cohosh (Caulophyllum Thalictroides)
- Pennyroyal (Mentha Pulegium)
- Neem (Azadirachta Indica)

PENNYROYAL

D

Demulcent/Mucilaginous

These herbs have sedative properties. They are mucilage rich plants, usually ingested to protect inflamed or injured mucous membranes in our respiratory system, gastrointestinal, or urinary tract.

Here are a few herbs that have demulcent properties:

- Aloe (Aloe Vera)
- Fenugreek (Trigonella Foenum-Graecum)
- Common Liquorice (Glycyrrhiza Glabra)
- Comfrey (Symphytum Officinale)
- Spiderwort (Tradescantia Virginiana)
- Marshmallow (Althaea Officinalis)
- Slippery Elm (Ulmus Rubra)
- Chickweed (Stellaria Media)
- Psyllium (Plantago Psyllium)
- Flax Seed (Linum Usitatissimum)
- Ox-Eye Daisy (Leucanthemum Vulgare)

MARSHMALLOW

Depurative

These are detoxifying herbs that eliminate toxins and waste from our bodies. These herbs have been in use for a long time, with people in olden times calling them blood cleansing herbs. These herbs were mainly used to treat chronic skin disorders, such as uncontrollable acne and musculoskeletal disorders as well.

Here are some herbal depuratives:

- Stinging Nettle (Urtica Dioica)
- Red Clover (Trifolium Pratense)
- Yellow Dock (Rumex Crispus)
- Cleavers (Galium Aparine)

Diaphoretic/Sudorific

These are medicinal herbs used to stimulate sweating in the body. Native Americans put a lot of importance in the process of sweating, believing it to be a healthy and cleansing process in our body. As sweating helps eliminate waste from the skin, it is believed that it purifies the body from most illnesses.

Here are some herbs that carry diaphoretic properties:

- Lemon Balm (Melissa Officinalis)
- Spearmint (Mentha Spicata)
- Catnip (Nepeta Cataria)
- Cayenne (Capsicum Frutescens)
- Elder (Sambucus Nigra)
- Safflower (Carthamus Tinctorius)
- Yarrow (Achillea Millefolium)
- Hyssop (Hyssopus Officinale)
- Peppermint (Mentha X Piperita)
- Blessed Thistle (Cnicus Benedictus)

LEMON BALM   CAYENNE   ELDER FLOWER   YARROW   PEPPERMINT

Digestive

These herbs act as digestive aids. They stimulate the digestive system to work properly and help promote easy digestion. They break down hard to digest foods so that our body doesn't have to work extra hard to perform the same function. Digestive herbs can be ingested as medicine or in the form of digestive teas.

Here are some examples of digestive herbs:

- Ginger (Zingiber Officinale)
- Yarrow (Achillea Millefolium)
- Sweet Flag (Acorus Calamus)
- Chamomile (Matricaria Recutita)

CHAMOMILE

Discutient

Discutient herbs are often useful in dissolving abnormal growth or tumors in the body. Even though it's not wise to treat cancerous growths with discutient herbs alone, some patients have reported that homeopathic remedies paired with allopathic medication has helped speed up the healing process remarkably, and many patients credit their tumors dissolving to these herbs.

Here are some examples of medicinal herbs that can dissolve tumors and abnormal growths in the body:

- Black Walnut (Juglans Nigra)
- Bloodroot (Sanguinaria Canadensis)
- Cabbage Leaf (Brassica Oleracea)
- Chaparral (Larrea Tridentate)
- Devil's Claw (Harpagophytum Procumbens)
- Garlic (Allium Sativum)
- Turkey Tail Mushroom (Triamedes Versicolor)

BLACK WALNUT

Diuretic

Diuretics are medicinal herbs that help increase the flow of urine. Usually, the term diuretic is used to refer to herbs that benefit the proper functioning of the urinary tract. People use herbal diuretics to treat obesity, to prevent and treat bloating caused by water retention and urinary tract infections. Diuretics are also useful in treating swollen lymph glands, skin rashes and even kidney stones.

Natural diuretics can be found in the following herbs:

- Dandelion (Taraxacum Officinale)
- Birch (Betula Spp.)
- Stinging Nettle (Urtica Dioica)
- Solomon's Seal (Polygonatum Biflorum)
- Bearberry (Arctostaphylos Uva-Ursi)
- Cleavers (Galium Aparine)
- Yarrow (Achillea Millefolium)
- Parsley (Petroselinum Crispum)
- Couch Grass (Agropyron Repens)

UVA URSI

E

Emetic

These are herbs that are used to induce vomiting and empty the stomach. These have been used throughout the ages to purge the body from poisons. They are still useful in case a person overdoses or consumes something toxic.

Here are a few examples of medicinal herbs with emetic properties:

- Knotweed (Polygonum Aviculare)
- Staghorn Sumac (Rhus Typhina)
- Pipsissewa (Chimaphila Umbellata)
- Pilewort (Ranunculus Ficaria)
- Twinleaf (Jeffersonia Diphylla)
- Milkweed (Asclepias Syriaca)
- Black Root (Leptandra Virginica)
- Bloodroot (Sanguinaria Canadensis)
- Vervain (Verbena Officinalis)

Emmenagogue

These herbs are used to stimulate menstruation. If a woman hasn't gotten her period on time, or wishes to induce it before time, these herbs can help. Emmenagogue herbs can stimulate blood flow into the pelvic area and the uterus, helping jump-start a woman's menstrual cycle.

Here are some examples of herbs that can help stimulate the menstrual cycle:

- Black Cohosh (Actaea Racemosa)
- Pennyroyal (Mentha Pulegium)
- Turmeric (Curcuma Longa)
- Gravel Root (Eupatorium Purpureum)
- Motherwort (Leonurus Cardiaca)
- Blue Cohosh (Caulophyllum Thalictroides)
- False Unicorn (Chamaelirium Luteum)
- Hibiscus (Hibiscus Rosa-Sinensis)
- Squaw Vine (Mitchella Repens)
- Juniper (Juniperus Communis)

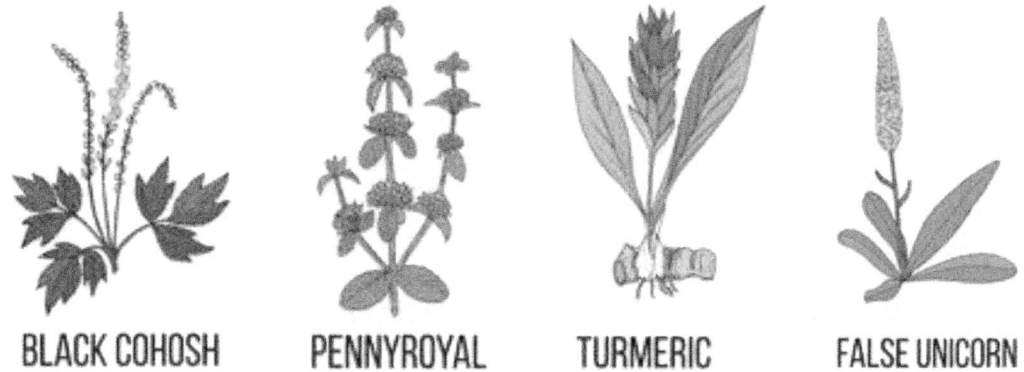

BLACK COHOSH   PENNYROYAL   TURMERIC   FALSE UNICORN

Emollient

These are herbs that are meant to be applied topically to the skin. They have a soothing effect and offer protective and healing properties against inflamed and irritated skin. They are only meant to be used externally and have properties which are similar to demulcents, only demulcents are consumed internally.

Here are some herbal emollients:

- Chickweed (Stellaria Media)
- Comfrey (Symphytum Officinale)
- Flaxseed (Linum Usitatissimum)
- Common Plantain (Plantago Major)
- Slippery Elm (Ulmus Rubra)
- Marshmallow (Althaea Officinalis)

FLAXSEED

Estrogenic

These herbs help regulate estrogen levels in the body. They often contain substances that the body can convert into estrogen as per required and are usually used to treat symptoms of menopause.

Here are some examples of estrogenic herbals:

- Angelica (Angelica Archangelica)
- Dong Quai (Angelica Sinensis)
- Motherwort (Leonurus Cardiaca)
- Wild Yam (Dioscorea Villosa)

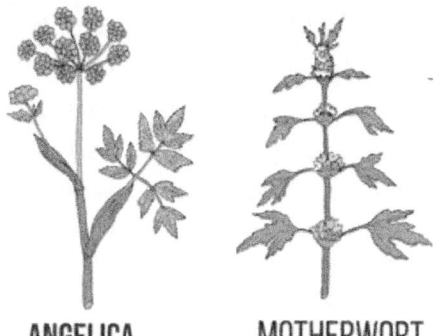

ANGELICA   MOTHERWORT

Expectorant

Expectorant herbs are used as medicine to stimulate secretion of excessive mucus from our lungs and airways. These herbs have the ability to change the viscosity of the mucus or by stimulating our cough reflexes to prevent it from clogging up.

Here are some examples of medicinal herbs that promotes the secretion of extra mucus from our lungs:

- Elecampane (Inula Helenium)
- Houndstongue (Cynoglossum Officinale)
- Coltsfoot (Tussilago Farfara)
- Fennel (Foeniculum Vulgare)
- Licorice (Glycyrrhiza Glabra)
- Eucalyptus (Eucalyptus Globosus)
- Common Mallow (Malva Sylvestris)
- White Horehound (Marrubium Vulgare)
- Great Mullein (Verbascum Thapsus)
- Wild Cherry Bark (Prunus Virginiana)
- Yucca Root (Yucca Schidigera)

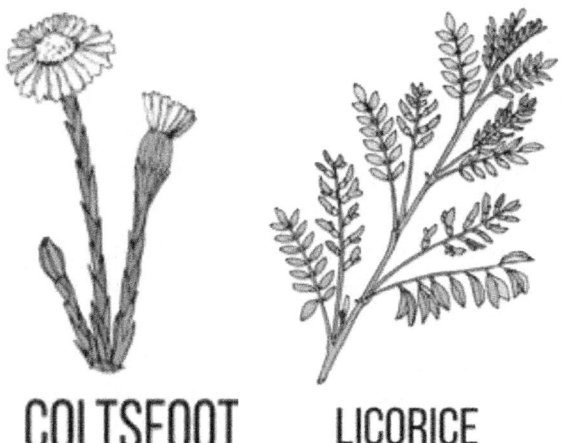

COLTSFOOT   LICORICE

F

Fungicidal/Antifungal/Antimicrobial/Antiparasitic

Fungicidal herbs do pretty much what the name suggests: they kill fungi and inhibit their growth. Fungi are pathogenic organisms that spread rampantly if not killed immediately, causing a whole host of diseases in the body. These herbs work either directly or indirectly; directly by killing the fungi, and indirectly by enhancing our immune systems so we produce enough antibodies to successfully eliminate the fungi ourselves.

Here are some examples of herbs that carry fungicidal properties:

- Marigold (Calendula Officinale)
- Mountain Laurel (Kalmia Latifolia)
- Tea-Tree (Melaleuca Alternifolia)
- Thyme (Thymus Vulgaris)
- Common Plantain (Plantago Major)
- Cornflower (Centaurea Cyanus)

CALENDULA

G

Galactagogue

These are herbs taken by nursing women who are unable to produce sufficient breast milk for their babies. These herbs stimulate the secretion of breast milk, enhancing its production and flow.

Here are some examples of herbs that increase the secretion of breast milk:

- Fennel (Foeniculum Vulgare)
- Anise (Pimpinella Anisum)
- Cleavers (Galium Aparine)
- Milk Thistle (Silybum Marianum)
- Red Raspberry (Rubus Idaeus)
- Goat's-Rue (Galega Officinalis)
- Fenugreek (Trigonella Foenum-Graecum)
- Milkworth (Polygala Vulgaris)

ANISE

H

Haemostatic/Styptic

Haemostatic herbs are used to stem the flow of blood. These herbs often carry astringent properties and help prevent or stop bleeding. They can be applied topically or ingested.

Here are some examples of herbs that can be used to stop bleeding:

- Yarrow (Achillea Millefolium)
- Tormentil (Potentilla Erecta)
- GoldenSeal (Hydrastis Canadensis)
- Common Oak (Quercus Robur)
- Knotweed (Polygonum Aviculare)
- Shepherd's Purse (Capsella Bursa-Pastoris)
- Bistort (Persicaria Bistorta)

YARROW   GOLDENSEAL

Hepatic/Hepatoprotective/Antihepatotoxic

These are herbs that can help make the liver stronger and protect it against diseases. These herbs also increase the secretion of bile, improving the health of the liver. Agents from these herbs are also used in synthetic medication to treat liver problems.

Here are a few examples of hepatic herbs:

- Milk Thistle (Silybum Marianum)
- Artichoke (Cynara Scolymus)
- Turmeric (Curcuma Longa)
- Dandelion (Taraxacum Officinale)
- Barberry (Berberis Vulgaris)
- GoldenSeal (Hydrastis Canadensis)
- Yellow Dock (Rumex Crispus)

MILK THISTLE

Hypertensive

Hypertensive herbs are very useful in helping increase dropping blood pressure. If you're suffering from low blood pressure, ingesting these herbs can help your blood pressure normalize.

Here are examples of herbs that can help increase low blood pressure:

- Licorice (Glycyrrhiza glabra)
- Black Cumin Seeds (Nigella Sativa)
- Hawthorn Extract (Crataegus)
- Celery Seeds (Apium graveolens)
- Flax Seed (Linum Usitatissimum)
- Garlic (Allium sativum)

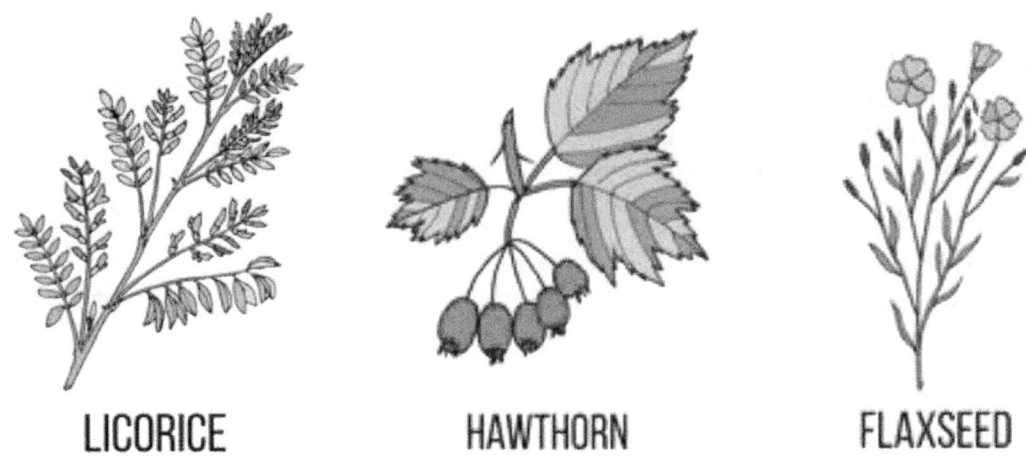

LICORICE   **HAWTHORN**   **FLAXSEED**

Hypoglycemic/Anti-diabetic

These herbs are useful for people that suffer from diabetes as they can reduce and regulate the levels of glucose in our blood.

Here are a few examples of hypoglycemic herbs:

- Fenugreek (Trigonella Foenum-Graecum)
- Neem (Azadirachta Indica)
- Goat's Rue (Galega Officinalis)
- Burdock (Arctium Lappa)

NEEM

Hypotensive

The opposite of hypertensive herbs, these herbs are used to regulate high blood pressure. If you are suffering from high blood pressure, these herbs bring your blood pressure back to normal.

Here are a few examples of herbs that decrease high blood pressure:

- Astragalus (Astragalus Membranaceus)
- Cramp Bark (Viburnum Opulus)
- Hawthorn (Crataegus Monogyna / Crataegus Laevigata)
- Mistletoe (Viscum Album)
- Linden (Tilia Cordata)
- Motherwort (Leonurus Cardiaca)

LINDEN

I

Immunosuppressant

Immunosuppressant herbs help lower the activity in our immune systems. These are especially useful for people who suffer from autoimmune diseases or have overactive immune systems.

Here are some examples of herbs that contain immune depressants:

- Indian Sarsaparilla (Hemidesmus Indicus)
- Asmatica (Tylophora Asmatica)

Immune-enhancing/Immune stimulant/Immunostimulant

Acting as the reverse of immunosuppressants, immune-enhancing herbs strengthen and stimulate our immune systems, making our bodies more capable of fighting off diseases and viruses.

Here are some herbs that carry immune enhancing actions:

- Astragalus (Astragalus Membranaceus)
- Chaga (Inonotus Obliquus)
- Echinacea (Echinacea Spp.)
- Wild Indigo (Baptisia Tinctoria)
- Neem (Azadirachta Indica)
- Cat's Claw (Uncaria Tomentosa)

ASTRAGALUS

L

Laxative/Purgative/Cathartic

These herbs are very effective at treating constipation. They work by facilitating bowel movements and stimulating the expulsion of feces from the body. Plants that carry strong laxative properties are sometimes called purgative or cathartic plants. Herbal laxatives are a great natural remedy for constipation, especially if synthetic medicine is not doing the job.

Here are some examples of herbal laxatives:

- Flaxseed (Linum Usitatissimum)
- Cascara Sagrada (Rhamnus Purshiana)
- Senna (Cassia Senna)
- Chinese Rhubarb (Rheum Officinale)
- Yellow Dock (Rumex Crispus)
- Solomon's Seal (Polygonatum Biflorum)
- Plum (Prunus Domestica, Prunus Americana)

Lymphatic System

Herbal lymphatic medicine is used to cleanse the lymphatic system. It stimulates our body's natural lymphatic system, causing it to work more effectively.

Here are some examples of herbs that stimulate our lymphatic system:

- Astragalus (Astragalus Membranaceus)
- Dandelion (Taraxacum Officinale)
- Poke Root (Phytolacca Decandra)
- Oregon Grape (Mahonia Aquifolium/Berberis Aquifolium)

OREGON GRAPE ROOT

N

Narcotic

Narcotic plants, though excellent at treating pain and coughs, have very addictive properties. Narcotic herbs also have an impact on the mood and behavior. They help induce sleep and also have psychoactive properties. Narcotics aren't the best for treatment options as some such as opium can cause terrible withdrawal symptoms if the body develops a tolerance for them.

Here are some examples of herbal narcotic plants:

- Indian Pipe (Monotropa Uniflora)
- Opium Poppy (Papaver Somniferum)

Nervine/Nervine tonic/Relaxant

These herbs naturally have properties that make people feel calm. They reduce feelings of anxiety and alleviate nervous tension that builds up in our body. They also strengthen our nervous system, making us more capable of bearing stress. These herbs can be ingested as medicine or as tea and can also be smoked.

- Peppermint (Mentha X Piperita)
- Skullcap (Scutellaria Lateriflora)
- Valerian (Valeriana Officinalis)
- Chamomile (Matricaria Recutita)
- Lady's Slipper (Cypripedium Acaulelemon)
- Lemon Balm (Melissa Officinalis)
- Catnip (Nepeta Cataria)
- Oat (Avena Sativa)
- Passion Flower (Passiflora Incarnata)
- Indian Pipe (Monotropa Uniflora)
- Cannabis (Cannabis Sativa)

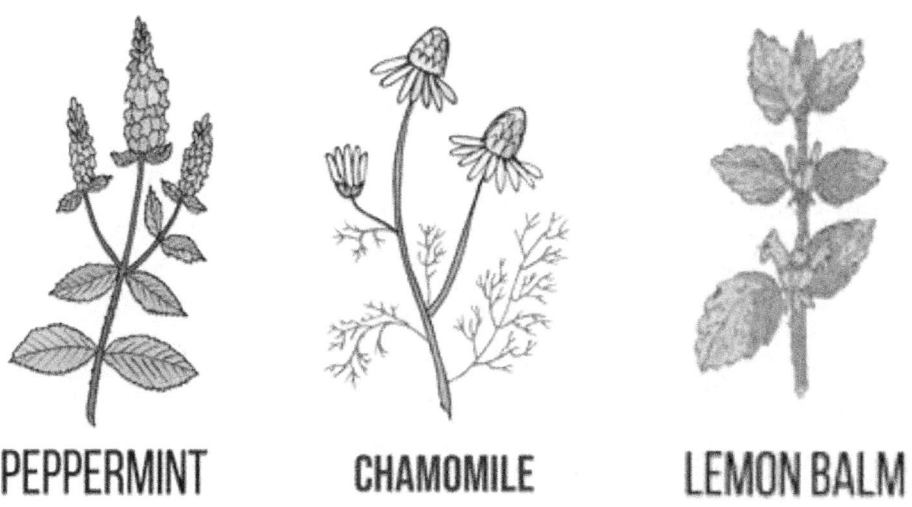

PEPPERMINT   CHAMOMILE   LEMON BALM

O

Oxytocic

These herbs are used to assist in childbirth. They stimulate uterine contractions, inducing labor. Midwives have used these herbs for ages, helping women in home births from the medieval times with the use of these herbs.

Here are some oxytocic herb that help in childbirth:

- Schisandra (Schisandra Chinensis)
- GoldenSeal (Hydrastis Canadensis)
- Blue Cohosh (Caulophyllum Thalictroides)
- Broom (Cytisus Scoparius)
- Shepherd's Purse (Capsella Bursa-Pastoris)

GOLDENSEAL

P

Parasiticide

These herbs destroy invading parasites that settle inside our digestive system or burrow their way into our skin. These parasites can be extremely dangerous and often deadly at times. Parasiticides help kill these parasites before they can do any lasting damage.

Here are a few examples of herbs that kill parasites in our bodies:

- Garlic (Allium Sativum)
- False Unicorn (Chamaelirium Luteum)
- Black Walnut (Juglans Nigra)
- Chaparral (Larrea Tridentata)
- Wood Betony (Stachys Officinalis)

GARLIC

Pectoral

These herbs help benefit our respiratory system by enhancing its function.

Here are some herbs that help enhance the function of our respiratory system:

- Coltsfoot (Tussilago Farfara)
- Elecampane (Inula Helenium)
- Great Mullein (Verbascum Thapsus)
- Marshmallow (Althaea Officinalis)
- Bloodroot (Sanguinaria Canadensis)
- Bunchberry (Cornus Canadensis)

Pediculicide

Pediculicides are herbs that are used in great natural remedies to kill head lice. Most modern medicines intended to kill head lice are considered to be harsh on the skin, and sometimes they are not as effective at killing these lice in one go. Some modern medicine even uses agents from these herbs in their formulas. These herbs can be applied topically to the skin in the form of shampoos and creams.

Here are a few examples of medicinal herbs that kill lice:

- Pawpaw (Asimina Triloba)
- Fir Clubmoss (Huperzia Selago)
- Tansy (Tanacetum Vulgare)
- Eucalyptus (Eucalyptus Globosus)

R

TANSY

Refrigerant

These herbs are applied to irritated, sunburned skin as it has a cooling effect. It soothes irritated and inflamed skin and can be applied topically in the form of ointments.

Here are some herbal refrigerants:

- Chickweed (Stellaria media)
- Chamomile (Matricaria recutita)
- Aloe (Aloe Vera)

ALOE

Rubefacient

These are medicinal herbs used to increase the flow of blood to the skin's surface. They also cause irritation on purpose, meant to draw out inflammation and congestion from deeper areas of the skin. These herbs are often used in remedies that are specially created to treat arthritis and rheumatism. These herbs can be rubbed onto the skin or ingested. They have been used for ages and are known to be effective.

Here are some examples of these herbs:

- Cayenne (Capsicum Frutescens)
- Horseradish (Armoracia Rusticana)
- Ginger (Zingiber Officinale)
- Thyme (Thymus Vulgaris)
- White Mustard (Sinapis Alba)
- Black Mustard (Brassica Nigra)
- Mezereon (Daphne Mezereum)

CAYENNE   THYME   GINGER

S

Sedative

Herbs with sedative properties are used to calm the nervous system and help alleviate nervous tension that builds up in the body. Some sedative herbs include antispasmodics and nervines. The purpose of these herbs is to help provide relief from pain, to help cramps subside, and to promote a restful sleep. They are also helpful for people who suffer from insomnia and high anxiety.

Here are a few examples of herbs that have sedative properties:

- Valerian (Valeriana Officinalis)
- Hops (Humulus Lupulus)

- Indian Pipe (Monotropa Uniflora)
- Chamomile (Matricaria Recutita)
- Yellow Jessamine (Gelsemium Sempervirens)
- Passion Flower (Passiflora Incarnata)
- Skullcap (Scutellaria Lateriflora)
- Lemon Balm (Melissa Officinalis)
- Lavender (Lavandula Angustifolia)
- Periwinkle (Vinca Minor)
- Catnip (Nepeta Cataria)

LAVENDER

Sialagogue

These herbs promote the production of saliva in our body. These herbs have properties that stimulate the rate of secretion of saliva in our bodies, helping promote the digestion of starch in the process.

Here are a few examples of herbs that perform this function:

- Pepper (Piper Nigrum)
- Cayenne (Capsicum Frutescens)
- Moneywort (Lysimachia Nummularia)
- Yellow Gentian (Gentiana Lutea)
- Ginger (Zingiber Officinale)
- Licorice Root (Glycyrrhiza Glabra)
- Blue Flag (Iris Versicolor)

Soporific

Much like sedatives, these herbs are also used to induce sleep. However, that is the only function they perform, they are not used to treat anxiety or any mood disorders. These herbs are just used to treat insomnia.

Here are a few examples of soporific herbs:

- Chamomile (Matricaria Recutita)
- Hops (Humulus Lupulus)
- Valerian (Valeriana Officinalis)
- Lady's Slipper (Cypripedium Acaule)
- Motherwort (Leonurus Cardiaca)

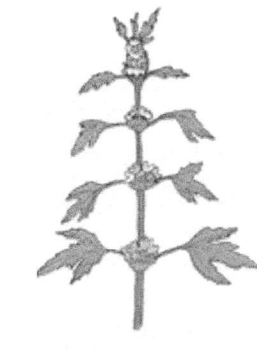

MOTHERWORT

Stimulant

The opposite of sedatives, these herbs enhance the functions of our organs, making us feel more alert and awake, giving us more energy.

Here are a few examples of stimulant herbs:

- Roseroot (Rhodiola Rosea)
- Cayenne (Capsicum Frutescens)
- Ginger (Zingiber Officinale)
- Peppermint (Mentha X Piperita)
- Asian Ginseng (Panax Ginseng)
- Rosemary (Rosmarinus Officinalis)
- Sage (Salvia Officinalis)
- Lemon Bee Balm (Monarda Citriodora)

CAYENNE   GINGER   PEPPERMINT   ROSEMARY   SAGE

T

Tonic

These are herbs that are used to create tonics, drinks, or potions that are meant to make our organs strong. These herbs nourish our organs and support their functions to promote overall health and wellness of our bodies.

Here are a few examples of herbal tonics:

- Asian Ginseng (Panax Ginseng)
- Roseroot (Rhodiola Rosea)

- American Mistletoe (Phoradendron Leucarpum)
- Dong Quai (Angelica Sinensis)
- Sarsaparilla (Smilax Aristolochiifolia)
- Astragalus (Astragalus Membranaceus)
- Stinging Nettle (Urtica Dioica)
- Dandelion (Taraxacum Officinale)
- Squaw Vine (Mitchella Repens)

SARSAPARILLA

V

Vasoconstrictor

These are herbs that act by constricting the blood vessels to reduce the flow of blood. This is useful for people who are on blood thinners or are bleeding uncontrollably to prevent excessive blood loss.

Here are a few examples of herbs that perform this function:

- Ma-Huang (Ephedra Sinica)
- Witch Hazel (Hamamelis Virginiana)
- Bugleweed (Lycopus Virginicus)

Vasodilator

Vasodilators serve as the exact opposite of vasoconstrictors. They expand and relax the blood vessels to allow increased blood flow throughout the body.

These herbs can be used as vasodilators:

- Ginkgo (Ginkgo Biloba)
- Horseradish (Armoracia Rusticana)
- Hawthorn (Crataegus Monogyna, Crataegus Laevigata)
- American Hellebore (Veratrum Viride)
- Linden (Tilia Cordata)
- Yarrow (Achillea Millefolium)
- Coleus (Coleus Forskohlii)

GINKGO BILOBA

Vulnerary

These herbs are used to treat wounds. They promote the healing of wounds by stimulating the growth of skin cells. These herbs are usually crushed up to release the healing agents and turned into an ointment or a paste to be applied topically on the skin. Most of these herbs also contain antibacterial and anti-inflammatory properties, so they help heal the skin faster and soothe irritated and broken skin.

The following medicinal herbs are known to vulnerary properties:

- Common Plantain (Plantago Major)
- Aloe (Aloe Vera)
- Sassafras (Sassafras Albidum)
- Solomon's Seal (Polygonatum Biflorum)
- Comfrey (Symphytum Officinale)
- Fenugreek (Trigonella Foenum-Graecum)
- Calendula (Calendula Officinalis)
- Marshmallow (Althaea Officinalis)
- Burdock (Arctium Lappa)
- Chickweed (Stellaria Media)

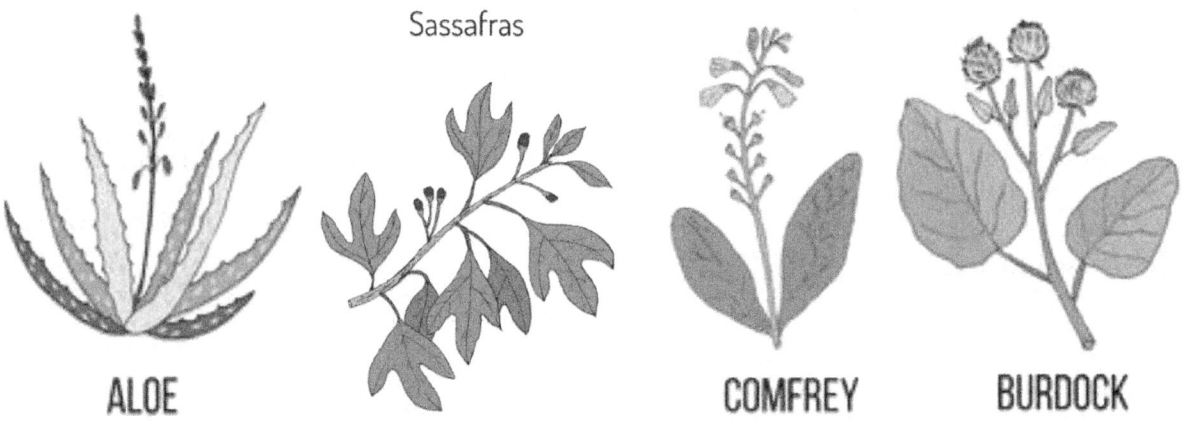

Sassafras

ALOE   COMFREY   BURDOCK

This is the complete encyclopedia of herbs. Hopefully, you can use the information you learned from this chapter to apply in natural remedies of your own creation. Do make sure that you conduct further research before creating any natural, herbal remedies of your own, as some of these herbs carry different properties which can react negatively with each other.

Make sure that you are aware of any allergies that you might have before creating these remedies for yourself to avoid any unpleasant allergic reactions. If you are creating ointments or creams, make sure that you test the recipe in batches. Apply a small amount of ointment on a patch of your skin to test it and leave it on for a specific period, like 15-20 minutes. If the ointment or cream has no adverse reaction, if you don't feel any burning, itchiness or redness, you may proceed to use it on the rest of your skin.

Never give any of the remedies that you create at home, which are untested, to children. Children are much more fragile than adults and face more extreme reactions. It is best to thoroughly research the properties and actions of each herb to make sure that they don't have any adverse reactions on your body. For example, an herb might have great anti-inflammatory properties but should not be used for people who have kidney disease. Make sure you keep an eye out for these things so that you don't end up doing more harm than good.

Lastly, it is always good to consult a medical professional before ingesting any herbal medicine. If you are using a tried and tested remedy that has been endorsed by reputable people, you can go ahead, but if you already have pre-existing health issues, getting a medical professional's opinion would help. It's always better to be safe than sorry.

Hopefully, you learned a lot from the encyclopedia of herbs. In the next chapter, we will discuss herbal preparations, which will teach you how to use these herbs in your remedies and recipes.

Chapter 4: Plants that Heal

Medicine today, no matter how evolved, still depends on plant products for healing. If at any point we doubted the effectiveness of past applications, the same plants exist in the ingredients of pharmaceuticals and drugs, albeit in a processed form.

Modern medicines are more specific in their treatments, and seemingly more effective, but often result in long-term side effects that need constant treatment. Perhaps it is for this reason that the modern-day pharmaceutical industry is a $484 billion self-feeding mechanism (Pharmapproach, 2020).

Currently, we have all the technology we can dream of, and the research methods, plus advanced levels of knowledge. We have inflated health insurance policies but yet the price we pay for healthcare is hardly reflective of our general health.

There is still a wide variety of herbs available today, possibly more than what the Native Americans had at their disposal. However, due to the lack of conclusive research, and the abundance of allotopic medicines, a small percentage is used in the form of medicine. This small percentage however translates to a large variety. Listed below are just a few.

Bloodroot (Sanguinaria Canadensis)

The Bloodroot plant is a uniquely attractive plant that hails from the poppy family (Papaveraceae) and gets its name from the red moisture in its rhizomes. It is also known as Bloodwort or its Algonquin name; Puccoon. They had a large degree of medical importance to the early Native Americans despite their high toxicity.

Description

The Bloodroot plant can reach a height of ten inches above the surface of the ground and its stems grow directly out of its rhizomes (Hobbs, n.d.). These rhizomes also sprout stems from both ends with the Bloodroot plant taking as long as three years to blossom (Mahr, n.d.).

Leaves

The plant has a single leaf that grows on a stalk that is separate from the flower and is an average width of between three and five meters wide and eight inches in circumference (Hobbs, n.d).

Flowers

The petals of the flower are white with discernable bright yellow stamens protruding from it. The flowers are about 1.5 inches in diameter, and relatively large for the size of the plant (ozarkedgewildflowers.com, n.d.).

Distribution

This plant thrives in damp soil with a low PH. It can be found growing in areas where there is enough shade to prevent the earth around it from drying out. For this reason, it is unlikely to occur in habitats like the flood plains, but rather in the wooded or thicketed areas of the eastern extremes of the North American continent. Bloodroot flower grows naturally from Nova Scotia in Canada down to Florida in the US.

Sanguinaria Canadensis tends to flourish in the late Winter and early Spring and in cases where they occur in the late Fall, their leaves will recede making them very hard to identify (Hobbs, n.d.). It can thrive in full sun but prefers partially shaded areas.

Ethnobotany

The Iriqous and the Chippewa used this plant for cloth coloring, basket dyeing, and face painting. It wasn't long before the European settlers cottoned onto the plant and adopted it for the same function to the extent that the French even started exporting it to dye wool.

The Ponca believed that when they applied it in a small dose to the palms of their hands and shook the hand of a maiden, she would be ready for wedding less than a week later (medicinalherbinfo.org, n.d.).

There are other cases where the plant was known to treat rheumatism and skin disorders (Davis & Greenfield, 2006).

Its early functions included treating harsh throat complaints and issues pertaining to the cardiovascular tract. It was also added to concoctions for ailments like heart complaints and migraines. The roots were dried and ground into a powder then applied to skin disorders like gangrene and worts (medicinalherbinfo.org, n.d.).

Contemporary Applications

Modern day research suggests that Bloodroot is capable of combating blood clots and that it has the potential to prevent the spread of breast cancer cells. While it shows promise the medical profession still doesn't have enough proof to take a formal stance on it.

Used correctly, the Bloodroot plant exhibits medicinal qualities. This is only when used in small doses. It is an effective treatment for rheumatism, congestion, sore throats, and respiratory conditions (Hallal, 2021)(nativeamericancultureblog, 2016).

Side Effects

Bloodroot is said to have been used as poison, as such it is noteworthy that Bloodwort is highly toxic if ingested. In cases where it needs to be taken orally, the doses have to be miniscule.

The general rule with Bloodroot and skin treatments is that it should not be applied to open wounds and sensitive areas like the genitals or around the eyes. It is corrosive and known to damage skin tissue, sometimes even scarring where used as a treatment.

Being a relative of the poppy it contains opioids and the leaves and seeds that form along its rhizomes are known to cause torpor and tremors (Barhum, n.d.).

Sanguinarine used to be an ingredient in many over the counter dental cosmetics to fight against dental plaque and oral bacteria. However, a link between the development of oral cancer and Sanguinarine has been discovered. It is for this reason that most toothpaste and mouthwash manufacturers are excluding it from their products, opting instead for disinfectants like doxycycline and chlorhexidine. Be this as it may, there are still oral hygiene products on the market that contain Sanguinarine (Flowers, 2013).

Chicory (Cichorium Intybus)

The wild Chicory flower, like the dandelion, is not endemic to North America but has played a role in Native American medicine for centuries. As a testimony to its true origins, there are reports of it being used by the Egyptians for its medicinal qualities and was even mentioned by Horace the Roman poet

(snaplant.com, 2015)(nativeamericancultureblog, 2016).

Description

The wild Chicory flower, like the dandelion, is not endemic to North America but has played a role in Native American medicine for centuries. As a testimony to its true origins, there are reports of it being used by the Egyptians for its medicinal qualities and was even mentioned by Horace the Roman poet (snaplant.com, 2015)(nativeamericancultureblog, 2016).

Flowers

The Chicory flowers are in full bloom during the day and close at night. They thrive from late in the Spring to mid Fall and grow as high as four feet and in rare cases may even occur in white or yellow (gardenia.net, n.d.).

Leaves

The fully grown leaves of the Chicory plant are thick and hairy and are between three and six inches long. In their infancy, they are oval-shaped and extend from the rosette structure at the base of the flower. These leaves are edible in the Spring but take on a bitter taste in the warmer months (Dodril, 2019).

Distribution

The chicory plant is not dependent on a lot of moisture and it can survive in dry conditions once they have matured. Due to its hardy nature, there are few places where it cannot be found in North America (Verdiell, 2020)(gardenia.net, n.d.).

Ethnobotany

Due to the color of this flower, the North Americans hailing from the eastern parts of the continent associated it with the sky. The entire plant is said to have been used to treat stomach, heart, and liver-related issues and the Cherokee used this flower as a nerve tonic (Ann, 2012)(native-languages.org, n.d.).

Unfamiliar with the coffee culture of Europe, indigenous Americans would make tea from its leaves and flowers. This brew served to relieve congestion associated with colds, sinusitis, and hayfever. The roots have a pungent taste and were used as either a substitute or an additive for coffee.

When used as a substitute by Euro Americans it was due to circumstances with the blockades imposed by the American Civil War.

Contemporary Applications

The roots of the Chicory plant can be boiled, sauteed, or caramelized, and the leaves make a tasty pot-herb or salad. To bring out a stronger taste, they can be roasted, and this is exactly the method employed when preparing it as a substitute for coffee (drugs.com, 2021).

Coffee may be one of the lesser evils but its caffeine content does have an impact on the body.

While the advantages of coffee are that it makes the mind instantly alert and minimizes the chances of oral infections, it also increases the chances of migraines, insomnia, and nervous conditions. Worst of all it is addictive to the point where one may develop withdrawal symptoms (Pietrangelo, 2017).

Chicory, on the other hand, while lacking that comforting dark color, bears none of the risks but instead a host of health benefits.

The Chicory plant is highly nutritious and contains inulin, which is a complex sugar helping digestive processes and staving off stomach issues. Chicory also contains antioxidants that help fight cancerous cells and promote a healthy gut. It is functional in the regulation of blood pressure and reduces the forming of platelets, thus making it good for the heart (drhealthbenefits.com, 2017).

Chicory is also considered a multi-purpose crop and it grows wild and free. Due to its increased market adoption, it is also cultivated and researched for its terpenes (essential plant oils) and inulin (chicproject.eu, 2020) (newsroom.idconsortium.com, 2020).

Its most common use in today's world is as an additive to coffee for flavoring.

Side Effects

The closest thing to a side effect associated with chicory is that it may be an allergen. Contact with skin can produce irritations. This allergy may then extend to the digestional tract if consumed. The latter is of course dependent on the individual.

The consumption of Chicory root by female rats is said to have produced contraceptive results. Researchers have noted that in certain cases it has even proved to be abortive. For this reason, caution should be exercised by women in any stage of menstruation, nursing, or pregnancy (nutrineat.com, 2010).

The Lady Slipper Orchid (Cypripedium Acaule)

An Obijwe tale speaks of a young maiden that made her way across the Winter snow in search of medicine for her sick and dying clan. Her mission was successful but in her plight, she lost her shoes yet she continued, even as her feet bled onto the snow. When Spring thaw came, flower-shaped moccasins grew out of her bloody footprints. These flowers are known today as lady slippers (Minogue, 2015).

The Lady Slipper Orchid is one of twelve species from the Cypripedioideae sub-family that is known for its unique shape (slipperorchids.info, 2020).

Description

The stems grow anywhere between 12 and 24 inches tall and the roots are coarse with rhizomes (britannica.com,n.d.-b).

Leaves

Two elliptical green leaves sprout from the base of the plant (basal leaves) and are arranged opposite each other. They are simple information and can grow up to six inches long with a width ranging between one and three inches wide. The leaves have fine hairs but are smooth to the touch (plants.ces.ncsu.edu, n.d.-a).

Flowers

The lady's slipper sprouts between one and two flowers that can grow up to three inches in size. These flowers have a unique shape due to their highly developed labellum (plants.ces.ncsu.edu, n.d.).

The flower lures pollinating insects past the external structures. Upon entry, the insect brushes against parts of the pistil and leaves traces of any pollen it's carrying on the flower's stigma. When the insect arrives on the inside and finds no pollen, it reverses back out. On its way out, some of the orchid's pollen rubs off on the insect's body. This pollen is positioned in a manner that makes it impossible for the insect to harvest (goorchids.northamericanorchidcenter.org, n.d.).

The nectar-pursuing insect, normally a bee, figures out the deceit and avoids the plant after that. This is one of the reasons that Lady Slipper has such a slow rate of replication (goorchids.northamericanorchidcenter.org, n.d.).

Distribution

The Lady Slipper Orchid occurs all over North America except Hawaii, Florida, and Nevada, and is cultivated throughout Europe for its ornamental purposes (britannica.com, n.d.).

Be this as it may, it has a slow reproduction rate. Nevertheless, the plant's status is considered to be secure (Minogue, 2015).

Ethnobotany

The Native Americans harvested the roots of this plant before and after winter. They found it effective for the treatment of labor pains during birth, menstruation, or headaches. Both

Native Americans and Euro-American doctors applied the plant exclusively to females for the treatment of anxiety, insomnia, and ailments where soothing was needed.

To the Native Americans, it is known simply as the moccasin flower. This was also used to treat pain, relieve sleeplessness, and because of its calming qualities, it was administered for nervous conditions like hysteria (Wei, 2012).

Native Americans would harvest the root, dry it out and then grind it into a powder. The resulting product is difficult to mix with water and thus at the time it was dissolved in liquids that took on solvent qualities, like alcohol (drstandley.com, 2021).

Contemporary Applications

The modern-day applications of the root of are as tonic for nervous conditions. The lady slipper is a slow working nervine that makes it an extremely safe natural treatment.

It also slows bleeding during menstrual cycles, pruritus, and any other instance where the body sheds blood, naturally or unnaturally (drstandley.com, 2021).

Side Effects

Since their oils constitute unstable compounds, their effects can be adverse. The lady's slipper orchid may result in skin irritation when touched.

It has the qualities of a sedative and thus excessive ingestion may lead to vertigo, headaches, restlessness, and sleepiness. For these reasons, pregnant or nursing women and those allergic to orchids should not use the treatment.

Lavender (Lavandula)

The Lavender bush, however, is not originally from North America and, much like the Dandelion, is suspected to have made its way across the Atlantic in the 1800s. This flower belongs to a genus of 47 species and is a member of the mint family. It is often mistaken for the Desert Lavender from the desert habitats of North America. The two are unrelated (native-languages.org, n.d.).

As with other introduced herbs, Native Americans became aware of them as they started populating the continent. As it gained ground, the Native Americans began associating the plant with purity and hygiene (nativeamericanherbalism.com, n.d.-b).

Since it was a later addition to their inventory, no mythology or folklore involves the shrub.

Description

It is an aromatic shrub-like plant with woody stems and purple, pink, or blue flowers (Kimbroug & Swift, n.d.). The most common species of this family in North America currently, is the Lavandula Angustifolia. It is better known by its common names: true lavender or English lavender.

Flowers

The flowers bloom in the summer and are usually a unique purple color where the name lavender purple comes from, though in some cases, these flowers may even be pink or white. These flowers can grow up to three inches in size and consist of four or five petals.

Leaves

The lavender is an evergreen plant with leaves that are a dull to silver-green color. They have a soft velvety texture and grow on opposite sides of the stems. These leaves are about an inch long, thin, and lance-shaped.

Distribution

Lavender is drought tolerant and thrives in grainy soils with a higher PH, and is exposed to a lot of sun. This makes Colorado ideal for the shrub. The plant is mostly cultivated and can be found in abundance in Washington State, New Mexico, and Texas.

Ethnobotany

By the time the Native Americans cottoned on to lavender, it already had an advanced following in Europe. Its functions, though broad, were mainly medicinal and used by European practitioners.

The Native American peoples brewed the herb in tea and used it to calm the body and mind (Jerrod, 2020).

Contemporary Applications

Lavender is effective in external applications and assists with muscle tension. It has a naturally occurring alcohol called linalool which acts as an antiseptic and when used as an ingredient of skin applications, it protects against bacteria. Linalool is a key ingredient in tonics that aid digestion (nativeamericanherbalism.com, n.d.).

Lavender is known for its fresh odor and as such it is used to create fragrances and household detergents. It can also serve a purpose in perfumes, flavorings, and tobacco (sagecreationsfarm.com, n.d.).

Recent research points at the species' potential to combat crop parasites and prevent the budding of potatoes in storage (McCoy, 2017).

Side Effects

Lavender teas usually contain a high percentage of lavender; as such, excess consumption of it can be disadvantageous.

It may also have adverse effects when used with medicines like barbiturates, chloral hydrates, antidepressants, or other sedatives. When it occurs as a tea, the excessive use of this herb can lead to breast development in boys. Among other symptoms, the herb can cause headaches, cold flushes, and emesis (Vilímovský, 2015).

Last but not least, it is a cross allergen, which means that while it is not an allergen per se, the body may react to it as if it were.

Violets (Viola)

Most species of violets are native to North America. They have an intense inclination to populate people's well-groomed lawns. It is for this reason that the plants are often considered weeds. The wild violet has a rich history in Native American culture

and was used for purposes that were both medicinal and decorative (The Survival Mom, 2019).

Description

Plants from the Violaceae family replicate either through the spreading of its root network or the dispersal of seeds. Violates can grow up to 10 inches tall.

Leaves

The leaves of violet species tend to take on an oblong, kidney, or oval shape. They grow on the same stem as the flower or separate stems. The average violet's leaves are just under an inch in diameter and are positioned on the stalk in an alternating formation (ediblewildfood.com, n.d.-b).

Flowers

Wild violets are typically purple, but may occur in different shades of blue, yellow cream, and even white and are generally between two and three inches in diameter. They are easily identifiable by their five heart-shaped petals with serrated margins and relatively large leaves (Landschoot et al., 2019). Violets generally have one flower per stalk (Josue, 2020).

Distribution

Violets are considered invasive and colonize favorable soil quickly with their rhizomes. They blossom around April and May, and their flowers turn to seeds in the off-seasons while their life retreats to their complex underground root networks. The violet thrives in moist, fertile soil, and cool humid weather (Landschoot et al., 2019).

Ethnobotany

The Haudenosaunee Nation believes that the violet is the offspring of the earth and the sky. For this reason, it is symbolic of balance and harmony (P, 2020a). To the Iriquois however, the plant is a symbol of love and bewitchment (native-languages.org, n.d.-e).

Native Americans used the flowers and the roots of these plants for medicines and dye (The Survival Mom, 2019).
The White Violet or the Violet Striata was infused in a cold tea to stop chronic vomiting and the roots were mashed and held against a sore tooth to make it fall out.

Salicylic acid, which is an ingredient of aspirin, is a naturally occurring compound in the Violet plant and thus it makes sense that the Native Americans crushed it into a poultice and used it for headaches (The Survival Mom, 2019).

Contemporary Applications

Violets have antibacterial properties and are an ingredient in ointments for bruises and scrapes. Their flowers are remedial for insomnia when brewed in a tea and when infused in an oil can be used to treat dermatitis, eczema, and other skin irritations. As a poultice, it can be applied to hemorrhoids and varicose veins. The leaves and flowers of the violet are edible and safe to use in salads (Blankespoor, 2016).

Side Effects

The roots, however, should be avoided as they can cause nausea and emesis (Blankespoor, 2016). While the body grows accustomed to the plant it may respond in the same way it would to a mild laxative, especially if consumed in large quantities. Aside from this, there are no known side effects to the viola plant (theherbalacademy.com, 2014).

Dandelions (Taraxacum)

These flowers arrived with the first Europeans in the 1600s but traveled faster on winds that scattered them across the plains and to the West coast of North America. The Dandelion colonized at a rate that made the Euro-Americans look like schoolboys (Krueger, 2019).

Its name is a mispronunciation of *Dent de Lion* which is French for tooth of the lion.

The daisy belongs to the Asteraceae family, a category that is shared by lettuce and sunflowers. It grows freely and like the violet, it is a tough flower to get rid of. It anchors itself firmly by its taproot, preferring newly cleared land above all (Anderson, 2017). In the modern-day garden, the dandelion is disliked and thousands of hours, kilojoules, and resolutions are committed to the eradication of the plant, yet they keep popping up.

Native Americans, being the master botanists, found multiple nutritional and medicinal uses for the plant (native-languages.org, n.d.-b).

Description

Its original name *Dent de Lion* comes from its leaves' serrations that are shaped like teeth. They are hardy species with taproots that run deep into the ground anchoring the plant firmly yet breaking up compact soils. In favorable circumstances, the plant can reach heights of up to 24 inches (Anderson, 2017)(plants.ces.ncsu.edu, n.d.-b).

Leaves

The average size of a leaf is eight inches long but in extreme cases, they can reach lengths of sixteen inches. They extend from a verticil or whorl on the surface of the ground and are bright green. Like the stem, if broken they secrete a milky white sap. All leaf lobes point towards the center stem and this is one of the easier ways to discern the difference between the dandelion and the chicory plant (Lindell, 2011).

Flowers

The bright yellow flowers are supported by a hollow stem and can reach a width of two inches wide. They bloom from early Spring up until late into the Fall and do so repeatedly throughout this period (Lindell, 2011).

Distribution

These flowers grow freely from Newfoundland to British Columbia and over two-thirds of the US. Dandelions favor medium to low altitudes and spring up in recently turned dirt or on lawns. This is no surprise as before lawns came into fashion these flowers were carefully arranged and manicured on the grounds of estates in Europe.

Ethnobotany

The Cherokee and Iroquois would chew on Dandelions to help with the pain caused by toothache.

The Ojibwas would boil the leaves and drink the tea which served the human body as an all-in-one wellness tonic. Kidney ailments, stomach pain, and heartburn were among the many disorders the herb was used to fix (Patterson, 2014).

Contemporary Applications

To the modern-day herbalist, the Dandelion is a diuretic, helps appetite, and eases digestion. It is a good source of vitamins A and C and is rich in Potassium.

This wild and free-growing flower is not limited to medicinal functions but can also be added raw to salads, sauteed, incorporated into soups, or fermented and turned into wine.

The trick with this flower is to get to it before its buds have opened, by doing it this way one gets to the leaves before they become bitter and inedible. The flowers and the roots of a dandelion are also fit for ingestion (poncatribe-ne.org, n.d.).

Brewed and consumed as tea, the dandelion will fight urinary tract infections, cleanse the liver, treat diabetes, avert chronic diseases, and improve digestion among other things (lybrate.com, n.d.).

Side Effects

Dandelions may act as an allergen creating swelling hives and in extreme cases anaphylactic shock.

Blood thinners, lithium, sedatives like valium, diuretics, and antibiotics may react adversely to dandelion treatments. As such, it is prudent to consult a physician before consuming dandelion with treatments for any of the above (Multum, n.d.).

Purple Coneflower (Echinacea Purpurea)

Echinacea belongs to the daisy family (Asteraceae) and is a relatively well-known prairie flower. Nine species prevail throughout the North American continent. They occur in the colors yellow, deep red, light pink, purple, and orange. Aside from these naturally occurring species, there are lab-developed cross breeds that produce numerous variants with striking colors.

Description

The name of the coneflower's genus Echinacea is derived from the Greek word Echino, which means hedgehog. This refers to the quill-like appearance of the spines in its cone.

The flowers and the leaves are propped up by a rather robust stem. The height of the plant ranges between 20 and 30 inches (bio.brandeis.edu, n.d.).

Leaves

The leaves of the purple coneflower are wide at the base, reach their width quickly and then taper off to a point more gradually. They are green with large teeth making the blades look serrated (bio.brandeis.edu, n.d.).

Flowers

When viewing the flower from the side, its petals seem to be drooping so far back that it exposes its stigmas, and if viewed from the top the flower seems to resemble the sun with the petals as rays.

Distribution

Echinacea is endemic to North America. While cultivated for commercial use, this herb still grows naturally in the areas on the seaward side of the Rocky Mountains in prairie-like habitats (webmd.com, 2011).

Ethnobotany

The purple coneflower is associated with elk and is often referred to as elk root. This association comes from the belief the wounded elk seek out Echinacea, the latter pays tribute to the ancient doctrine of signatures (Cassaro, 2011). This is an example of how the Native Americans learned from their animal counterparts and assimilated these lessons into their lives (native-languages.org, n.d.-b).

The Native Americans who hailed from the great plains, commonly known as the Plains Indians, were well acquainted with this particular plant because of their shared locations. The Navajo considered the Echinacea to be a sacred plant.

Archaeologists believe that the Sioux of the 17th century used Echinacea to treat syphilis. The first Euroamerican account of the herb was by John Clayton of the mid to late 1600s when he wrote of using it to treat the sores on horses caused by saddles (spiceography.com, 2019).

The roots of this flower have a history of being used to treat pain, swelling, and inflammation among the Native Americans of the Plains and the Midwest. It is chewed ritualistically during ceremonies like the sweat lodge and the sundance.

The functions of the plant differed among the first nations. The Sioux used the herb to treat tonsillitis and bowel disorders while the Cheyenne, Kiowa, and Comanche applied it to oral sores like toothaches and inflamed gums, sore throats, and coughs (spiceography.com, 2019b).

Echinacea enjoyed formal advocacy as early as the 19th century. The Eclectics delved into phytopharmaceuticals and made echinacea a key ingredient of most treatments during that period (Hobbs, n.d.).

Contemporary Applications

Echinacea is available over the counter in a fresh form and can be brewed as tea. It is also sold as an oil infusion, cream preparation for the skin, squeezed as a juice, and used as an extract in capsules (Wilson, 2020).

Today it is cultivated to feed the demand and dominates the herbal remedy world (healthyfocus.org, 2016).

Echinacea is also used in treatments for gonorrhea, septic diseases, hydrophobia, and colic (Hobbs, n.d.).

Side Effects

Echinacea is generally safe for ingestion by adults, but the impact on nursing or pregnant mothers is still unknown. The most common side effect of echinacea is stomach cramping, bowel movements, or allergies. Be that as it may, these issues rarely occur and this makes echinacea a safe form of herbal treatment in adults (nccih.nih.gov, n.d.).

Indian Tobacco (Lobelia Inflata)

This plant also goes by the name of Puke Weed or Bladder Pod Lobelia and belongs to the Bell Family (Campanulaceae). It is a lot prettier than the name suggests. How it tastes, however, is a different story, and it contains lobeline which has similar effects to nicotine and as we know, this is the key ingredient in tobacco. Though now known for its function as either chewing or smoking tobacco, it is a noxious weed and can have fatal results if ingested in sizable amounts.

Description

The Lobelia Inflata is a herbaceous annual with a simple upright stem bearing fine hairs (wildflower.org, n.d.). At full maturity, the plant can reach heights of two feet and a width of one foot wide. It is a hermaphrodite and thus bears both sexes which allows it to self-fertilize.

Flowers

The lobelias' tiny flowers vary between different shades of purple and in certain instances are even white. They are bilaterally symmetrical and each one has five petals. In each flower, there are five stamens (gobotany.nativeplanttrust.org, n.d.).

The fruit of the tobacco plant which can range from six to eleven millimeters is dry in texture and opens up when it is ripe (gobotany.nativeplanttrust.org, n.d.).

Leaves

The leaves of the plant are simple in type. This means that they are unbranched and have no natural separations like that of the dandelion. They also alternate on the stem and are limited to one per node. The lobelia inflata leaf edge is serrated and thus rough to the touch (gobotany.nativeplanttrust.org, n.d.)(toddcaldecott.com, n.d.).

Distribution

The lobelia inflata species favors terrestrial surfaces but are occasionally found in wetlands. It grows naturally in most parts of North America and thrives in open woods, waste areas, and gardens (healthyfocus.org, 2016).

Ethnobotany

The indigenous of North America also valued the plant for its medicinal qualities. The early European settlers assumed that because it was smoked, it was tobacco, but unlike anything else the indigenous clansmen would smoke, this was done for health purposes to deal with lung issues.

It was also used by the Shoshone for its emetic and cathartic qualities while other accounts hint at its ingestion for the treatment of gut parasites and syphilis.

It was used as a poultice to treat headaches among the Cherokee. Euro-American doctors of the 19th century used it to induce vomiting, this was the same method employed by the Native Americans to treat alcoholism (herbrally.com, n.d.).

The American indigenous found use for the herb to deal with whisky addiction that was the fall of many a cultured individual. It was rumored that if snuck into the food of a couple who fought often, the herb would reignite their love for each other (altnature.com, n.d.).

Other uses both recent and historical are as a treatment of lung diseases, cardiovascular disorders, and the removal of mucus and phlegm from the bronchioles (Haw, 2017).

Contemporary Applications

Lobelia can be used internally and externally and has stimulating and soothing effects. As mentioned before, it contains an alkaloid known as Lobeline. For this reason, lobelia occurs in products and supplements that are intended to suppress tobacco cravings. The use of this herb extends to the treatment of alcohol addiction and is administered to help cure hangovers (Gregutt, n.d.).

Lobelia today may be used in mixtures with other herbs like Lungwort, Coltsfoot, Grindelia, Ephedra, and Skullcap. In homeopathy, it can be applied to heart disorders, dizziness, and cardiovascular symptoms (Gregutt, n.d.).

There has also been research into the herbs capabilities to treat psychostimulant addictions. While its taste has proven to be the biggest hurdle, it has shown potential against the effects of methamphetamines on the brain (onlinelibrary.wiley.com, 2016).

Side Effects

Like with all good things, too much of it is a bad thing, so much so that the Australian government has banned the use of it for human ingestion. The side effects of incorrect or overuse are:

- Lightheadedness
- Queasiness
- Low Blood Pressure
- Vomiting
- Trembling
- Incoherence
- Indolence or Paralysis
- Coma
- Death (altnature.com, n.d.)

Witch Hazel (Hamamelis Virginiana)

The word 'witch' in its current name comes from 'wych,' which is of Germanic origin and refers to its flexible bark. The trunk of this tree and its main branches tend to be grey in color while the twigs are a reddish brown.

As a testimony to the latter, the Native American

used its branches to make bows (illinoiswildflowers.info, n.d.).

Description

Witch hazel, also known as tobacco wood, winter bloom, or snapping alder can grow to a height of 20 feet and is considered a small tree or large shrub.

The tree's base will reach a width of approximately one foot in diameter at maturity (illinoiswildflowers.info, n.d.).

Flowers

The witch hazel blooms in the Fall and produces a yellow flower when it does. Flowering occurs from October to December and this tends to be after the tree has shed its leaves. Its flowers form on the higher branches of the tree and each one has four long petals. These flowers will eventually fade away and woody acorn-like structures will begin to form.

From beginning to end the fruit takes a year to develop and will signal its ripeness by exploding and ejecting its contents (the seed) up to 20 feet away. This will precede the new blooming season (missouribotanicalgarden.org, n.d.)(illinoiswildflowers.info, n.d.).

Leaves

The asymmetrical leaves tend to be roughly oblong or oval and are on average five inches long and three across. They are green in the summer but turn a golden yellow in the Fall. Their distribution across the stems alternates while their blades have wavy edges (illinoiswildflowers.info, n.d.).

Distribution

Witch hazel grows wild along the eastern side of the continent covering roughly a third of the width. These trees thrive in environments with a moderate amount of moisture, where there is intermittent sunlight and shade. The witch hazel favors soils from those that are sandy in texture to those that have a moderate amount of clay (illinoiswildflowers.info, n.d.).

Ethnobotany

The Osage used the bark of this plant and its leaves in the form of a poultice and applied it to swelling, skin sores, and inflammation and the Iroquois regarded it as an all-around restorative. They also brewed it and applied it internally and externally for heavy menstrual bleeding, open wounds, fever, tumors, and eye irritations (Andriote, 2012)(encyclopedia.com, 2013).

Contemporary Applications

Witch hazel's medical functions are multiple and its applications include the treatment of hemorrhoids, swelling, oral inflammation, varicose veins, and burn wounds. The use of the plant is also recommended in the tincture form for the treatment of sunburn, insect bites, pulled muscles, and plant-induced irritations of the skin like that caused by poison ivy.

The active agent in witch hazel is Hamamelis, which is extracted from its dried leaves, bark, and branchlets via means of decoction, tinctures, or distillery.

Recent research has shown that the plant is high in antioxidants and because of its astringent capabilities, it can numb irritated areas and stop bleeding while minimizing the potential for infection (encyclopedia.com, 2013).

Today extracts of the plant occur in gels, creams, and ointments such as Preparation H (encyclopedia.com, 2013).

Side Effects

The tannin content of this shrub may result in adverse stomach reactions like pains, and ingestion of as little as one gram may lead to emetic behavior, difficulty when passing stools, and dizziness. It is noted that the combination of blood thinners or alkaloids and witch hazel have adverse effects (encyclopedia.com, 2013).

Witch hazel contains safrole which belongs to the methylenedioxybenzene group of compounds. These compounds are prevalent in insecticides. While minuscule doses of witch hazel can be ingested with visible health benefits, the continued use of it may have long-term side effects like cancer (Miller et al., 1983).

Yarrow (Achillea Millefolium)

The yarrow flower is native to many Northern Hemisphere countries and belongs to a genus of 140 different species (Nemeth & Bernath, 2008). It has a long history among the Native Americans for whom it served as an all-purpose remedy. Its medicinal strengths were recognized by early civilizations throughout the world and its healing powers in the modern-day world are undisputed.

Description

The yarrow is a resilient perennial that can grow up to three feet in height. Due to its leafy nature, it takes on the appearance of a fern. It is favored for its showy flowers and thus thrives in gardens like xeriscapes that don't get a lot of water.

Flowers

Its white five-petalled flowers grow in flat-topped inflorescence and appear from April to October. They vary in color according to species and can occur in the colors white, yellow, red, and orange.

Leaves

The leaves are small and resemble the structure of a feather and as the name Millefolium suggests, there are many leaves (cabi.org, n.d.).

Distribution

Yarrow is a circumboreal flower, meaning that its native habitat falls within the temperate regions of the Northern Hemisphere. Be that as it may, it occurs throughout North America (Rey-Vizgirdas, n.d.).

Ethnobotany

There are suggestions that this plant was introduced to North America. Given the prevalence of it in Native American folklore and how many of the indigenous nations have names for it in their languages; any allegations of it being an introduced plant are dubious.

Historically it was used as a poultice and applied to headaches, pains, and intestinal complaints. To the Navajo, it holds sacred value as a medicine and to the Anishinabe, it is burned as a purifying herb (native-languages.org, n.d.-e).

Native Americans used this plant's leaves for scenting and sometimes combined it with other perennials when washing their hair (Wolf, n.d.). It also served as an astringent and hence instrumental in the treatment of wounds, inflammation, and skin complaints (Amy, 2020).

Contemporary Applications

Yarrow is rich in flavonoids which is a natural chemical that triggers the flow of saliva and enzymes. This is due to its bitter taste and as such, it is helpful for the body's digestive processes. It is also useful in the prevention of colds and flus and their treatment; this is because it minimizes the buildup of saliva and mucus and causes perspiration. In doing so, it helps the body secrete toxins (Amy, 2020).

It occurs in treatments for ailments that affect the liver and also possesses hepatoprotective qualities. It is a diuretic, anti-inflammatory, antispasmodic, emmenagogue, and antimicrobial.

Side Effects

Its side effects manifest as sleepiness, the constant need to urinate, slow blood clotting, and uterus contractions. For these reasons, it is advisable to avoid yarrow when using Lithium-based medicines, during pregnancy, breastfeeding, or while on blood pressure treatment (Dellwo, 2020).

Hawthorn (Crataegus)

Hawthorn, being a member of the rose family, is a thorny shrub with woody stalks and distinctive white flowers which along with its fruit and leaves is used to make medicines. The berries have additional uses and feature in jams, wines, and sweets.

The hawthorn bush thrives easily

almost anywhere in the world and is often kept for ornamental reasons. It is capable of long life (400 years) in ideal circumstances (P, 2020).

Its importance to the early Native Americans aside from the belief that everything possessed spiritual value, was mainly medicinal, and in so saying, its function differed from clan to clan. Irrespective of what it was used for, it was effective.

Description

The hawthorn bush is a deciduous tree that is dense in its growth and is likely to reach a thirty-foot height (D, 2011).

Flowers

The hawthorn tree's white flowers are referred to as Mayflowers when they occur in the spring. When the resulting berries ripen they turn a reddish color and the taste is a combination of sweet and sour.

Leaves

The leaves of this plant are between 1.5 to 2.5 inches long and dark green (fs.fed.us, n.d.).

Distribution

Like the yarrow bush, this tree thrives in the temperate regions of the Northern Hemisphere. Today it can be found in the northeastern corner of the US overlapping into the south eastern extremes of Canada (fs.fed.us, n.d.).
The hawthorn bush favors deep damp soils that are of fine grain and thus will be found along rivers and streams, hence its prevalence in the British Columbia area.

Ethnobotany

The Potawatomi nation used the berries of the bush for stomach pains while the Ojibwe made a broth from it to treat loose bowels. For the Chippewa, the roots served to address female ailments.

Aside from these functions, there were multiple other applications by the Native Americans both internal and external including the Kwakiutl who chewed the bark and then applied it to skin wounds (Foster, n.d.).

Contemporary Applications

Its main use in modern medicine is for heart diseases as it helps to widen the blood vessels and thus the heart is then capable of pushing out more blood when it contracts. For this reason, it is instrumental in cholesterol and the treatment of diabetes.

Side Effects

For safety reasons, any treatments that affect the heart or the blood and blood pressure should not be used in tandem with hawthorn products as the herb tends to alter the circulatory system. Caution needs to be practiced when there are pre-existing disorders like weak erections among men and diabetes. In these instances, a physician should be consulted before using treatments containing hawthorn (webmd.com, 2019).

Adverse reactions to the plant include irregular stomach behavior, pains in the chest, heart palpitations, nausea, irritability, insomnia, excessive perspiration, and dermatitis. Individuals who are allergic to roses should avoid hawthorn (webmd.com, 2019).

Elderberry (Sambucus Canadensis)

The elderberry, which goes by many names, is a fast-growing shrub. Its historical use by the first nations was to quell stomach ailments and ward off evil from infants. In today's world, the berry is still widely used to address stomach complaints, and for its nutritional value.

Description

The elderberry plant has woody stems and grows to an average height of about 15 feet.

Flowers

In June, the shrub sprouts numerous clusters of small white flowers that give way to a deep purple fruit which is poisonous to both humans and animals unless cooked.

Leaves

The elderberry's leaves are of a compound structure and have a saw tooth ragged edge. They are roughly oval, dark to olive green, and lighter in color on their undersides. Each leaf is about ten inches long (ediblewildfood.com, n.d.).

Distribution

The elderberry thrives in loamy soil and semi-shaded environments. It occurs from north to south along with the eastern coastal areas of the North American continent (fs.fed.us, 2019).

Ethnobotany

Native Americans used the thorns on the branches to prick blisters. These thorns seconded as fish hooks for the indigenous peoples living along the coast. The berries and the bark are believed to have been effective against running stomachs. The flowers were used to protect babies from unwanted energies and illnesses (splitrockenvironmental.ca, 2013)(wildfoodsandmedicines.com, 2014).

Contemporary Applications

Modern-day research shows that elderberry has the propensity to fight cancer, sinusitis, hay fever, and improves the immune system by increasing the white blood cell count. It helps to protect against the sun's ultraviolet rays and research also suggests that this plant may be a diuretic. Last but not least, animal testing has indicated that the elderberry improves moods giving it potential as an antidepressant (Mandl, 2018).

Side Effects

The elderberry contains chemicals known as lectins which occur in most uncooked organic foods. These chemicals exist mostly in healthy foods. The ingestion of the latter may result in leaky gut syndrome, weight gain, immune system malfunctions, and resistance to natural insulin. Fortunately, by cooking the elderberry the lectin content is depleted (Mandl, 2018).

Cyanide also occurs in the fruit in small doses but exposure to heat through cooking does away with it. Children under the age of 18 and women who are lactating should abstain from elderberries, and when setting out to harvest special care should be taken to ensure that the correct berries are harvested. There are numerous species of elderberry and many of them are toxic whether they are cooked or raw (Mandl, 2018).

It should be noted that other parts of the elderberry tree are not fit for consumption. Common reactions to elderberries are dizziness, vomiting, stupor, and disorientation (Mandl, 2018).

Uva Ursi (Arctostaphylos)

The uva ursi is an evergreen shrub that is native to North America. It is also known as the bearberry and this is since it is favored by bears. It is better known by its traditional name; Kinnikinnik and when occurring independently they become very dense.

Description

The plant grows up to eight inches high and has woody but flexible branches that are earthy brown, often to the point where they have a reddish tinge.

Flowers

The flowers are white and blossom between May and June but are replaced by red berries when they wither away.

Leaves

The leaves are positioned alternatively on their stems. They are elliptic in shape with a glossy upper surface. They are dark green and can grow up to 1.25 inches in length.

Distribution

Uva ursi enjoys widespread distribution from as far north as Alaska and all along the eastern extremes of the continent into the California area. The uva ursi is also prevalent across the northern extremes and along Pacific Ocean coastal areas and the Atlantic seaboard. It is widely distributed across most of Canada.

The uva ursi favors rocky soils but can be found in habitats like woodlands and beaches too (Christiansen, 2020)

Ethnobotany

Not only was this plant used for medicines among the Native Americans but to the Bella Coola natives it was an ingredient to a traditional dish made of melted goat fat, this dish was of a high value as it was intended for their chiefs. The Blackfoot ate it the same way or in a mashed, dried, or fresh form. The Chippewa and the Cheyenne mixed the leaves with tobacco and smoked them.

Other Native Americans mixed it into grease and applied it to skin conditions. The Carrier nation uses it with fish eggs to create a meal with high nutritional value (wnps.org, n.d.).

Contemporary Applications

The plant's leaves are sold over the counter as a tincture or in crushed or powder forms. The berries are rarely used in modern-day remedies. The leaves are the most popular part of the plant and are formulated for internal use and external applications.

Uva ursi plays a role in combating water retention and urinary tract infections. It may also serve as a hepatotoxin and disinfectant for the kidneys.

Side Effects

Continued use of the plant over longer than two weeks is not advised. Larger than necessary doses are likely to result in adverse effects that include emetic body reactions, sleeplessness, vertigo, irritability, and a telltale sign would be a greenish tinge in the urine.

Internal use of the herb should be avoided when lactating or pregnant. The long-term effects of misuse are damage to the liver, kidney, eyes, and respiratory system (herbwisdom.com, n.d.).

Wavyleaf Thistle (Cirsium Undulatum)

The wavy leaf thistle is a relative of the sunflower. It belongs to the Aster family and the Cirsium genus which are considered true thistles. It is the most common thistle native to North America.

This species is one among the many similar-looking perennials that prevail and this makes it a difficult job to distinguish it from its counterparts. The wavy leaf thistle contains both male and female organs and thus it is a hermaphrodite.

This plant is said to be one of the more palatable thistles known to humankind; the roots and stems can be eaten cooked or raw (naturalmedicinalherbs.net, n.d.).

Description

It consists of diverging stems that grow to an average height of two feet. It is spiky and hairy in appearance which gives it an unapproachable look.

Flowers

The process leading up to flower development can take as long as ten years. As is characteristic of thistles, the wavy leaf is a hardy plant entity and can survive unfavorable growing conditions for years. After the flowers are formed, the plant will die as it commits all its resources to the seeds that form in the flower. Be that as it may, few of these species make it to the blossoming stages.

It sports purplish-pink or white corollas which protrude from a spiny base. These flowers occur as one or more per stalk.

Leaves

Their leaves are hairy which gives them a silvery appearance with spines protruding from their margins. The leaves of this plant can reach lengths of up to ten inches (ag.ndsu.edu, n.d.-a).

Distribution

They are prevalent across a large area of the US, covering the western half of the continent from North to South. They also extend into Mexico and Canada and prevail in random pockets in some of the country's eastern states. The Wavy thistle can thrive in most types of soils with a neutral to alkaline PH (pfaf.org, n.d.).

Ethnobotany

Native Americans used these plants to treat STDs (sexually transmitted diseases). They would brew it and make the patient drink it as tea and then induce sweating. Males with the condition were required to do a grueling run and then cover themselves in a blanket. If the infection occurred in a female she wouldn't need to do the run but just sit in a blanket until she started perspiring. There are accounts of the roots being boiled in a soup or for the treatment of diabetes and minor stomach qualms (ag.ndsu.edu, n.d.).

The roots were also soaked in water and then used to rinse out the eyes to treat infections (temperate.theferns.info, n.d.).

Contemporary Application

Its modern-day uses are similar to its historical functions especially with regards to the treatment of gonorrhea and eye complaints. Aside from this, the plant is still ongoing research.

Side Effects

It contains a high percentage of inulin which is a complex sugar that cannot be digested by the human digestive system. This then results in flatulence. Other than this, there are no other known side effects.

Mormon Tea (Ephedra Nevadensis)

Mormon Tea is part of the Ephedra family that consists of botanical bush species with needle-like branches. This name was given to the plant because the Mormons used it for tea. It was a substitute for coffee due to their staid version of Christianity that prohibited their intake of caffeine. The resulting action was then to infuse the twigs with hot water. Little did they know, this bush had a high percentage of nerve stimulants called ephedrine. The effect of ephedrine on the human nervous system is far more potent than that of caffeine (encyclopedia.com, n.d.).

Mormon tea has a remarkable effect on the body; it dilates the breathing tracts and raises the heart rate in the same way adrenaline would.
This was not the first time that humans found a use for the plant. Before the arrival of the religious sect, the Native Americans had already discovered its effects. Variations of the species also occur naturally in Europe, Asia, and South America (encyclopedia.com, n.d.).

Description

The Mormon tea bush is a spiny little clump that is off-yellow to light green and grows up to four feet tall.

Flowers

They have flowers with male and female reproductive parts which occur on separate plants. These flowers are formed in the first four months of the year.

Leaves

This bush appears to have no leaves, but they do exist as ultra-small spikelets at the joints of these plants.

Distribution

The Mormon tea bush takes to the semi-arid fields and habitats of New Mexico, Utah, and Arizona. They can also be found in woodland areas. Mormon tea gravitates to areas that get full sun and is resistant to extreme weather, hot or cold (Charlie, 2010).

Ethnobotany

The Native Americans also prepared the plant as tea but way before the Europeans set foot on American soil. The White Mountain Apache, among many other first Nations with access to it, used the spines to treat STIs (Sexually Transmitted Infections). The Kawaiisu would char the spines and use them to tattoo themselves while other Native Americans used them to deal with diarrhea (texasbeyondhistory.net, n.d.).

Contemporary Applications

The qualities of Ephedrine and Pseudoephedrine went mostly unknown until the 1970s. It then started occurring in sports supplements to such an extent that WADA (World Anti-Doping Agency) has resorted to banning it in quantities that are more than 10 mcg per milliliter of body fluids (encyclopedia.com, n.d.).

Another application is as a nervous system stimulant in weight loss products. With the increase in heart rate and blood pressure comes suppression of appetite, but with this comes the risk of myocardial infarction. Thus it has been banned by the FDA (Food and Drug Administration) (encyclopedia.com, n.d.).

Unfortunately, dietary supplement producers outside the US still include Ephedrine in their products (encyclopedia.com, n.d.).

Side Effects

The side effects of Mormon's tea may include but are not limited to nasal and throat cancer, liver and kidney damage, hyperactive bladder functions, and constipation. Ephedrine minimizes the body's absorptive functions and thus when used in concert with any other treatments or medicine, the medicines' effects will be minimized (emedicinehealth.com, n.d.).

Cattail (Typha)

Typha also goes by the names punk, bulrush, reedmace, and Sausage Tails among others, and belongs to the Typhaceae family. They are erect perennials that have a complex network of rhizomes with tender edible starchy innards. The roots of these reeds are high in nutrition  and have the potential of food sources that are comparable to other grassy crops like maize, flour, oats, and rice (The Editors of Encyclopedia Britannica, 2018b).

Description

Cattail grass needs to have its lower regions submerged for most of its life to achieve maximum growth. In favorable circumstances, the riverine species replicates quickly. It maintains a deep matt green color when in its prime, and when it dries out it becomes a golden yellowish to light brown.

The cattail stalk comprises multiple different nodes that can grow up to nine feet tall.

Flowers

The tiny flowers on these unisex reeds develop on the rather large spike, and when they are ready, they travel in the wind to their destinations and pollinate. The male flowers are positioned above the opposite sex. Once they shed their pollen their purpose is fulfilled and they wither away. The fertilized females then take on a brownish color and disconnect from the matriarchal cattail where after the seeds form and are then distributed wind (The Editors of Encyclopedia Britannica, 2018b).

Leaves

The leaves are tapered, an inch wide, with smooth edges, and populate the stalk in a scattered fashion.

Distribution

The cattail is semi-aquatic and can be found along inland bodies of semi brackish and freshwater. The current status of the plant is "invasive" as it proliferates throughout the country.

Ethnobotany

To the Native Americans, this plant was a source of clothing, ornaments, food, and medicine. The rhizomes when crushed made a good poultice and served to deal with any breaks or disorders in the skin. The "fluff" or the spikelets that are also referred to as flowers were used as gauze on open wounds, the juice from the leaves as an antiseptic for the skin, and the sap of the stem for pain relief (ncnativeethnobotany.org, n.d.).

For the Mescalero Apache, the cylindrical section of the plant played a role in the females coming-of-age ceremony; for other Native Americans, the roots and leaves were treatments for stomach pains (ncnativeethnobotany.org, n.d.).

Contemporary Applications

It is healthy for the skin and the jelly substance that it produces can be topically applied to acne, boils, rashes, minor insect bites, and other irritations.

The gel-like substance that lives between the leaves can be applied to vulnerable areas like grazes, cuts, and sores. The plant also has analgesic value and through ingestion, it can relieve pain and inflammation. The cattail is a coagulant and thus when applied to hemorrhaging it will slow the bleeding. It is helpful to treat excessive menstrual blood loss (lybrate.com, 2020).

From a nutritional perspective, the cattail makes a good all-purpose survival food. The roots can be dried and ground down to make baking flour, and the shoots and roots can be eaten raw or cooked.

Cattail stalks can be used as a material for building shelters.

Side Effects

The cattail plant is one of the milder species in the plant kingdom and thus the side effects are minor. It is prone to cause uterus contractions and pregnant women should steer clear of it.

It may also contain allergens or cross-allergens. Sometimes it is known to cause a loss of appetite. Since cattail is a coagulant, it is not an optimum choice of herbal treatment for individuals with blood circulation issues (lybrate.com, 2020).

Staghorn Sumac (Typhina Rhus)

Sumac plants exist in subtropical and temperate areas throughout the world. Sumac belongs to the Rhus genus which has 250 flowering species, 35 of which are native to North America (Myers, n.d.).

One of the most common species is the typhina rhus. This plant possesses a wide variety of healing and nutritional qualities and serves many purposes in the modern kitchen, as well as in herbal and medicinal inventories.

Description

The staghorn sumac is the largest of the Native American variants and occurs in tree or shrub form. It gets the name stag's horn from the shape that its smaller branches take on. These new branches are covered in reddish-brown hairs that give them a satiny texture. The staghorn sumac can grow up to 25 feet tall (missouribotanicalgarden.org, n.d.-a).

Flowers

The rhus typhina blooms between June and July and the male and female flowers occur on separate trees. The females grow in hanging clusters that become crimson-colored berries in the Fall and prevail throughout the winter (Hitz, 2019).

Leaves

The leaves are large, green (lighter on their undersides), and of a pinnate structure. Each leaflet is about 5 inches and the compound leaf can reach lengths of up to 24 inches (missouribotanicalgarden.org, n.d.-a).

Distribution

The staghorn thrives in almost all types of soil and can be found alongside roads, on the embankments along railroads, next to bodies of fresh water, and on the edges of forests in areas that are exposed to full or medium sun (missouribotanicalgarden.org, n.d.-a).

The natural distribution of this plant occurs throughout the eastern part of North America.

Ethnobotany

Early Native Americans used the roots and leaves of the staghorn sumac as an astringent, for the purification of blood, to induce vomiting and the passing of urine. A tea brewed from the bark was used to treat numerous female conditions including the production of breast milk. Infusions were also used to fix stomach disorders, and the inner bark was used to treat hemorrhoids and prolapsed uterus (naturalmedicinalherbs.net, n.d.).

The berries of this plant were served in teas for sore throats and blood cleansing purposes.

Contemporary Applications

The fruit of this tree is soaked in cold water to produce a refreshing drink. Should the resulting infusion be boiled it will trigger the release of acids which will then make it an astringent (Stag's Horn Sumach Rhus typhina, n.d.).

Side Effects

There are no known side effects, documented or otherwise. There have however been accounts of the plant's fluids creating skin irritations (herbpathy.com, n.d.).

Mint (Mentha Arvensis/Canadensis)

Colloquially, the herb is known as American or Canadian mint. It belongs to the sage or dead nettle family and is part of a genus of 25 different species (britannica.com, 2021). The plant has a distinctive menthol taste and smell.

Certain literature may depict it as the same thing as mentha arvensis, which is wild mint. The two have close characteristics but the Canadensis species can grow much taller (30 inches and higher). The key defining feature between the two is the distribution of the mentha arvernensis. It is circumboreal, making it native to the northern temperate zones.

Description

The mint plant has a hairy stem that can reach up to 18 inches in height (gobotany.nativeplanttrust.org, n.d.-b). The plant is perennial and has a creeping network of rhizomes that produce shoots, which then become separate plants growing on the surface of the soil.

Flowers

The flowers form at the top of the stem notes between the petioles and the stems and are purplish, pink to light red, or white. These flowers bloom in July and August (eattheplanet.org, 2021).

Leaves

The leaves are striking deep to light green, of an ovate shape, and are supported by a short petiole. They are positioned opposite each other in sets of two per node along the stem. The edge of the leaf is serrated and ovate with the tips tapering to a sharp point (gobotany.nativeplanttrust.org, n.d.-b).

Distribution

It grows in the north-western areas of the continent down to Mexico in the South preferring wetland habitats because of its dependency on water (eattheplanet.org, 2021).
Variants of this species can be found in Southern Africa, Australia, and Eurasia.

Ethnobotany

Native Americans used mint leaves to treat bad breath, hiccups, in poultice form to treat pneumonia, and as an all-round tonic. They also used the plant as bait for foxes and lynxes (primidi.com, n.d.).

Its cousin Mentha Arvensis had more specific applications: Mint leaves were chewed to help treat sore throats and the entire plant served as a galactagogue. It was also an anti-inflammatory and a pain reliever that was used as an ingredient of infusions. These infusions served as an emetic, proved remedial for stomach complaints. The plant was effective in the treatment of colds (treeandlandscapecompany.com, 2021).

Contemporary Applications

It has a key function in flavoring foods especially in candy and teas (eattheplanet.org, 2021).

The medicinal uses for plants belonging to the Mentha genus are broad. In the form of oil infusions, they are remedial for external applications like muscle and nerve pain. The plant itself is effective in the treatment of stomach qualms.

Research has shown that the mint can fight different kinds of bacteria and thus they have potential in the treatment of cancers and influenza. It is also an apt treatment of stomach complaints.

Side Effects

Oils or external infusions with a high mint percentage should be used in microdoses. Excessive exposure can cause headaches and skin irritations. Consumption of the plant in quantity will affect the liver adversely. People with a deficiency of stomach acids, gallbladder malfunctions, acid reflux, and esophagus complications should abstain from mint.

Wild Ginger (Asarum)

Wild ginger belongs to the Bitworth family and grows close to the ground. It is the only plant in its genus and has no connection to commercial ginger root. It is a slow grower, but in optimum circumstances will proliferate rather quickly.

Description

The average wild ginger plant grows to the height of ten inches and width of 24 inches (hgic.clemson.edu, n.d.).

Flowers

The off-red flowers form on the stems below the leaves attracting insects that pollinate them when they bloom in the early months of spring. The flower's color and smell is that of decaying carrion and thus draws the same insects that pursue animal carcasses. The latter echoes another instance of the relevance of the doctrine of signatures (fs.fed.us, 2019b).

Leaves

The leaves are dark green, kidney or heart-shaped, and glossy. According to the prehistoric doctrine of signatures, the leaves hinted at the plant's medicinal values. They grow from opposite sides of stems that rise from the rhizomes in pairs (hgic.clemson.edu, n.d.).

Distribution

The wild ginger plant thrives in moist fertile soils of a neutral PH. They prefer shady locations and are thus common in woodland habitats. They occur naturally from the northern extremes of North America to the south and are prevalent across the western half of the continent (fs.fed.us, 2019b).

Ethnobotany

The roots were dried and burned as insect repellent. They were also boiled for long periods, the resulting infusion would then serve as a contraceptive to the Native American nations. As a decoction, it can be used as an antiseptic, herbicide, and deodorant among other things (Jackson & Bergeron, n.d.).

The roots were served in syrup or candied to treat stomach pains (Strauch, 1995). The Meskwaki nation poured the sap from the rhizomes into ears to heal earaches. Ginger was also used as a spice to treat meat when it was from an unknown source, and preserve it (wp.stolaf.edu, n.d.).

The flowers and the stems of the asarum are toxic and thus not fit for ingestion in any form.

Contemporary Applications

Medical research has determined that the plant has antibiotic qualities. Ginger is used in drugs and treatments for breathing and bronchial conditions like clearing phlegm migraines and dehydration (rxlist.com, n.d.).

Side Effects

The wild ginger plant has been known to cause skin irritations (sciencedirect.com, 2014). The only time it is safe for consumption is when it is free of aristolochic acid (occurs naturally). The plant would require processing to achieve this.

Aristolochic acids occur in the bitworth family and while it does have uses in the treatment of gout and arthritis, its biggest danger is in its continued use.

Ingested in large amounts, even free of aristolochic acid, Assurum can induce vomiting, dizziness, diarrhea, and even paralysis. With continued use, it can damage the kidneys and cause cancer. Thus it is best used as a flavoring in foods and sparingly as a medical treatment.

The use of the asarum by pregnant women may cause miscarriage as it is known to trigger menstruation. There is not enough research available on the effects it is on nursing mothers and their young and to remain safe it should be avoided (rxlist.com, n.d.)

Wild ginger has a relaxing effect on the colon and thus it is not a good digestive, for this reason, it is not ideal for after meals. Infants and young children are intolerant to it as it results in the epiglottis obstructing the airway and likely to cause gagging (herbal-supplement, 2014).

Roundleaf Greenbrier (Smilax Rotundifolia)

The greenbrier is a climbing vine from the greenbrier family. Small filaments grow off the vine which eventually anchor it on its host or a convenient surface. Being a wild species they are difficult to keep in check.

They can grow into dense impregnable thickets and to the untrained eye, they may resemble ivy. If not identified early the greenbrier family is inclined to overwhelm other garden plants. They are often thought of as weeds and great efforts are taken to eradicate them (Joe, 2019).

The berries are an inky dark blue with large seeds in them allowing for minimal edible material. When they ripen some detach from the vine, but a fair amount of them remain on the vine and are capable of surviving the winter providing food for animals who remain active throughout the cold months (Joe, 2019).

The greenbrier vine, though indigenous, is considered an invasive plant. It can spread quickly has deep rhizomes, this makes it fire proof.

Description

It grows in untidy bunches and the plant's woody stems have thorns on them that are spaced a few inches apart and project off the stem at a 90-degree angle. These thorns are approximately a third of an inch in length. The light green vine doesn't exceed more than a quarter of an inch in width (Joe, 2019).

The stems tend to maintain a diamond-shaped cross-section (Kent, n.d.).

Flowers

The typical greenbrier flower is white and forms on a growth that extends from points on the vine where the stems and the petioles diverge (the axel). They bloom in the transition between spring and summer. Male and female flowers are approximately the same size, a third of an inch, and are produced on different vines. These flowers form in clusters of between 20 and 30. After fertilization, the female flowers become greenbrier berries (jungledragon.com, n.d.).

Leaves

The greenbrier has lustrous green heart-shaped leaves which are between 2 and 2.5 inches from the start of the petiole to its tip. Each leaf has between three and five veins spreading from its base to the blade.

Distribution

There is a large population of them in the east and southeastern parts of North America. They grow alongside roads, in wooded areas, and clearings and if left unchecked, will become a dense impassable thicket (jungledragon.com, n.d.).

Ethnobotany

Native Americans used the plant to treat toothache by holding a piece of root against the offending spot. It has also been used to clear and loosen mucus, stimulate bladder functions, and trigger bladder movements (Kneller, 2021). Teas made of the roots were drunk to purify the blood and a hot leaf infusion helped to dispel the afterbirth.

Contemporary Applications

The new spring shoots are edible as is the vine provided that the thorns haven't hardened and turned woody yet.

The more commonly known use of the plant is of its roots in culinary dishes. The roots make a tasty substitute for asparagus and the tendrils like the leaves make a good ingredient for salads. The sap of the roots also serves as a thickening agent (jungledragon.com, n.d.).

Side Effects

The plant has no known side effects.

Chapter 5: Herbal Preparations

Once you've mastered the properties of herbs, the next step is to figure out how to use your knowledge of herbs in herbal preparations so you can put it to good use. There are many ways that you can use herbs to create remedies and recipes that serve different beneficial purposes.

There are various ways to prepare herbal remedies, each with their own sets of pros and cons. These methods have been meticulously developed over the ages through a tedious process of trial and error and have been used by human beings for health and wellness purposes for centuries.

Herbalists have explored the magic of herbs and discovered that each part of a plant has its own specific healing powers. Each of these powers have different levels of potency in different forms. Some herbs for example, work best if used in oils while others prove to be more effective in tinctures and potions. The form you prepare your herbal remedies, is very impactful in determining its effectiveness.

It's always a good idea to do your research before creating your own herbal remedies. While this book is a pretty effective guide, it wouldn't hurt to do some extra research to make sure that you're not making any mistakes and mixing any herbs that are not supposed to go together. It takes a lot of patience, trial, and error to figure out which method of preparation works best for which herb and what should be the amounts and dosage you mix in for maximum effectiveness with no detrimental effects.

A good way to do this, apart from online research, is to visit local herbal stores or health food stores to see how they package specific herbs. Similar herbs will be grouped together in shelves, so you would know that they share common qualities and actions. You can also read the recommended dosages on the label to know how much you are supposed to safely consume.

In this chapter, you will learn what constitutes different herbal remedies and get tips on how you can make these remedies and recipes by yourself at home. Each method has a different level of potency, which will be mentioned, so you can tell which is the strongest and fastest acting and which are gentler versions of the remedies.

The measurements can vary based on use, but make sure you don't pass the recommended dosage. Research the strength of the herbs you are using and their effects beforehand. Don't use any herbs that you are unfamiliar with because you would have no idea how they react with others.

The part of the herb that you use also makes a big difference. The leaves, roots, stems, seeds, and flowers all carry different actions, so you might need to adjust the amount you are using in accordance with the part of the herb.

A good rule of thumb to go by is to generally use one ounce of any singular herb, or one ounce of combined herbs. If you are using fresh herbs, you would need to use twice the amount as you would dried herbs.

You can make these herbal preparations using either dried or fresh herbs. If you have the space, consider growing your own herbs to save money. If you develop a keen eye for herbs, you can even wild-craft them; pick them up from the wild. However, you would need to be extra careful while picking wild herbs because it's very easy to make a mistake and pick something deadly instead. For example, it is very easy to mistake deadly nightshade for jimson weed and poisonous toadstools for edible mushrooms. If you're unsure, the best thing to do is to buy your herbs from your local health food store.

One thing to remember when deciding which best herbal method you should use to prepare your herbs, is to decipher how you can get the herbs you want as close to the area of the body where you need them to work through as efficient means as you possibly can. For example, if you have a splinter in your foot, you wouldn't consider drinking herbal tea to see if it can pop out as a result; you'd work on getting the splinter out directly by yourself. You'd analyze the area; the splinter is on my foot, I can pull it out using a pair of tweezers. A similar principle applies to working with herbal remedies as well. For instance, if you have a headache, you can make a soothing and pain relieving poultice that you can apply directly on the forehead for pain relief.

You must remember that herbal remedies don't usually work like taking prescription medications, and rarely would you ever see immediate effects. However, they do work slowly because they have gradually acting properties. You would need to continue to use the remedy to see eventual results. If you're using your remedies in the form of teas, make sure you're drinking the teas until you see a change in your condition; same goes for other remedies as well. It usually doesn't take longer than three days, so be patient. The time it takes to come into effect also depends on your body type, so it's different for everyone.

How effective our herbs are depends on how well their gradual action restores the natural balance of your body's natural, healthy functions. It is very seldom that herbal remedies are capable of producing long lasting beneficial effects after just one dose. You need to continue taking the remedy to have long lasting results.

If you are treating a chronic problem with herbal remedies, generally it would take a month of herbal treatments to treat each year that you have suffered from the problem. For example, if you have suffered from chronic backache for five years, it would take at least five months of herbal remedies to treat that problem in a healthy way.

When you're making herbal preparations using medicinal herbs, you need to make sure that any treatments that you consume are prepared fresh every day. This rule doesn't apply to herbal salves, ointments, liniments, and tinctures, as you can keep them stored properly for longer periods. It would be for the best to keep things as simple as possible to avoid overcomplicating things and risking an adverse reaction. Try using one herb at a time in the beginning until you get the hang of things and you can combine different herbs effectively.

As there are so many different types of preparation methods, measurement is incredibly important. Overusing any medicinal herb can be detrimental to your health, so it is essential that you learn how to properly mix your solutions; this is a cardinal rule of alternative medicine.

Remember, the goal here is to produce remedies that can have a long lasting, beneficial effect on your body, making you healthier and promoting a state of wellness. You have to take care while using herbal remedies because it is very easy to overdo them. Prescription and chemical medicine have stronger action, and usually doctors prescribe specific amounts that need to be consumed. As herbal medicines have slower action, you have to consume them regularly over a long period to see results. Getting impatient and taking more will be more detrimental than beneficial. This is considered to be abuse of herbal remedies and must be avoided at all costs. Anything done in excess is dangerous for us. People assume just because something is natural, it is safe; that is not always the case.

One thing to remember is to never make herbal preparations in aluminum pots and pans. This is really important and must be considered before preparing your home remedies.

It is very easy to get overwhelmed by the amount of medicinal herbs available and all of their different properties and all the varieties of preparation methods that you can potentially use. Here is a list of some common, yet effective, methods of herbal preparations that you can use to create your own herbal remedies at home.

Infusions

Infusions are usually liquids like teas, prepared by using medicinal herbs that dissolve easily in water or slowly release their active ingredients in oil. An infusion is created to draw out the most sensitive and fragile healing properties of an herb. They are often created using the softer parts of a plant, usually the leaves and the flowers. This can differ from herb to herb; for example, for herbs like Goldenseal and Valerian, the root is used instead of the leaves or flowers.

The process of making an infusion is pretty straightforward. All you have to do is pour boiling water over a specific herb and let it steep for about 15-20 minutes, or until the mixture cools down. Then you have to strain the mixture, separate the herb from the liquid, then bottle it up, and store it for future use. Some infusions can be refrigerated, while it is recommended to keep other infusions in cool, dark places. You can also add honey for additional benefit and to enhance the flavor if you want. Some people like adding honey and lemon as well. The most common proportion used to create herbal infusions is using one ounce of herb to one pint of liquid

The purpose of using boiling water is to slowly extract the healing properties of the herb from its parts. The water slowly releases vitamins, sugars, enzymes, and some volatile oils, along with tannins, saponins, bitter compounds, glycosides, and other proteins. Boiling water also helps release polysaccharides in the herb, along with pectins and some alkaloids as well.

Infusions are usually just considered to be teas. However, you can create both hot and cold infusions, each have their own distinct properties and benefits.

Hot Infusions

Hot infusions are created in the following way:

1. Put a teaspoon of dried herbs or two teaspoons of fresh herbs in a cup
2. Pour a cup of boiling water on the herb
3. Cover the cup and let it steep for 10 minutes or until the mixture is cool

These are basic guidelines that you can adjust according to how much you need, or you can adjust it according to your taste as well. You can adjust the amount of herbs you use in order to make a pint of the infusion. If you want to make the taste stronger, make the mixture more concentrated by adding more herbs and letting it steep longer, or if you want to make the taste mellower, dilute the infusion with more water and use fewer herbs.

Cold Infusions

Cold infusions take the longest to prepare out of all the herbal remedies that use water. Cold infusions are created by submerging herbs into cold water for a long period, at least forty eight hours. Since in hot infusions, the healing properties of herbs are drawn out by heat, in cold infusion, the process takes longer for the agents to diffuse into the water, and as a result, the infusion is much milder than herbal teas.

Here are the steps you can follow to create a cold infusion:

1. Take a bowl or cup and fill it with cold water (You can use cold water from the fridge, some people prefer using steam distilled water for utmost purity).
2. Steep the herb and keep checking every four hours. The concentration of the mixture will depend on the herb that you use. You might have to leave it for a period of two to three days.
3. You can store your infusion either at room temperature or the refrigerator.

Sun Teas

A sun tea is a happy medium between hot and cold infusions. They are considered to be very refreshing, soothing, and healthy. Like other herbal teas, they are easy to prepare and get absorbed fairly quickly by your body.

Here is how you can create your own sun tea:

- Prepare the herbs just like you would in a hot infusion
- Instead of pouring boiling water, pour room temperature water in your container
- Tightly cover the container with a lid (mason jars would be the best for this)
- Leave your container on a sunny window sill or outside in the sun
- Your sun tea will be ready in four to eight hours

Most people are no strangers to infusions. Many cultures have recipes for medicinal herbal teas in the family; you can even find weight loss teas on Instagram that promote flatter bellies. If you have ever had any kind of tea before, then you've definitely had an infusion. These mixtures are called 'infusions' because the herb is submerged into water to draw out its healing properties and medicinal compounds. The beneficial agents from the herbs are 'infused' into the water.

Usually herbal infusions are created using the most delicate parts of the herb because they break down and dissolve easily. Usually these consist of leaves and flowers as mentioned earlier, but infusions can also be created for things such as mosses, corn silk, and lichens.

Apart from boiling water, you need certain tools to create your infusions. You can find these tools around the kitchen, such as a tea-strainer or cheesecloth. You can consume your infusion hot or cold; the preparation doesn't matter. You can refrigerate a hot infusion and drink it cold or warm up a cold infusion and drink it like that. Usually, it is recommended to consume infusions as soon as you make them, but some infusions can be stored if refrigerated for up to a week.

Teas

Herbal teas are basically hot infusions. They are pleasant to consume and incorporating herbal tea into your diet is a healthy decision. Most herbal teas have a mildly relaxing or refreshing effect. They can make you feel mellow or invigorated, depending on the properties of the herb. However, herbal teas are not as potent as other ways of making herbal preparations.

You can easily make medicinal teas at home. You can store loose tea leaves, or make your own tea bags using dosages according to your preference. You can then steep them in boiled water for 10 minutes whenever you want to consume them. You can also create a medicinal tea using normal tea that you can buy at the store; just triple the amount that you use. By tripling the normal amount, you can come very close to getting the medicinal value of an infusion. You can consume certain herbal teas as many times as you like during the day without detrimental effects. However, make sure that the properties of the teas do not cause any excessive symptoms. For example, it is not a wise idea to consume excessive cups of laxative herbal teas.

If you are preparing your herbal tea from dried herbs, measure the bulk of them and toss that quantity into a non-metallic container. It is smart to have a kitchen scale handy to measure how many herbs you are supposed to add to your tea. The recommended dosage, as mentioned before, is one ounce. Usually people drink herbal teas at room temperature. Consuming very hot tea will benefit you only if you want to induce sweating or are suffering from a cold or cough. Consuming hot green tea for weight loss is also beneficial. You can sip the tea whenever you feel like; the advisable dose would be about one to four cups, but that depends entirely upon the herb you are consuming.

Here are some pros and cons for consuming infusions:

Pros

Out of all the herbal remedies, infusions are the easiest to prepare. All you need are the herbs and water. Infusions are mostly pleasant to consume and because they are mild, they don't have many adverse effects. It is easier for herbs to release their medicinal properties into water than other substances, for example alcohol, which is the base for tinctures. For example, if you are using raspberry leaves, they will release more medicine in hot water than they would in alcohol. The best way to find out which herbs will work best in your infusion is by conducting research. Your research will tell you which herbs will best benefit you, and will bring out the most in your infusion.

Cons

Even though infusions are fairly simple to make, not everybody appreciates the taste of different herbs mixed together. This holds true especially if you are using astringent and bitter herbs. You might feel like gagging before consuming the teas brewed from these herbs; adults might have a hard time choking these down, let alone children. However, there is a really easy way around this.

The potency or effectiveness of these infusions will not be impacted if you add things to enhance their flavor. You can always add honey, agave, maple syrup, brown sugar, or lemon to your infusions to get rid of the bitter taste and make the tea easy to drink. However, not all herbal teas have the same problem. Some herbal teas actually taste really good and are quite pleasant to drink.

Decoction

A decoction is similar to infusions. It is a method where herbs are lightly boiled to release their healing properties. Unlike infusions, decoctions can include stems, bark, roots, and rhizomes of an herb. Infusions are usually made from the leafy, delicate bits of an herb, while decoctions can be made using the harder parts of the herb.

Decoctions are usually made in a non-metallic container, where the herbs are simmered with water as it comes to a boil. If you are using roots for your decoction, the simmering process could take up to one and a half or two hours.

To create a decoction, you would need to add one ounce of dried herb (hard parts) or two ounces of fresh herb parts to one pint of water. You need to chop up the herb as finely as you can and place the contents in a small pot, along with the water. It is preferred to use a stainless steel, glass, or enamel pot to create a decoction instead of an aluminum pot.

To make the decoction, you would need to simmer the herbs in the water, until the water comes to a boil. Once it comes to a boil, you need to turn the heat as low as possible and reduce it, bringing it to a simmer for at least 20 minutes. Then, you need to strain the liquid as well as you can use a cheesecloth. For best results, you can wrap the cheesecloth around a colander to drain the liquid as well as possible. Pour the liquid into the cup and drink it while it's warm.

Decoctions use the same amount of herbs as an infusion so you don't have to differ much based on that. Make sure you use a container that has a tight fitting lid to store your decoction. Once again, a mason jar would be the best container to use. The simmering process usually takes 20 minutes, but it can take longer depending on the herb.

You can drink your decoction after it cools, or you can allow it to steep overnight, then strain and drink it in the morning. Try not to store your decoction for too long; it's best to consume as soon as it's cool enough to drink.

If you compare a decoction to an infusion, decoctions require a longer time for extraction, using consistently hot and simmering water on the stove. Since decoctions are made from the thicker, more resinous material from a plant, this method is the best to get the healing properties out of the herb. Since infusions are created using the more delicate parts, they are considered to be milder than decoctions. One exception to this rule is when you are making a solution using a nettle leaf. To create a herbal remedy using nettle leaf, you would want to use an overnight infusion or a light decoction for best results.

Herbs have specific properties, so some work better with infusions while others work better as decoctions. It depends on what nutrients you are hoping to extract from the herb. Some herbs might be suited more to cold or overnight infusions as hot water can actually destroy some healing properties in certain herbs. You can do research online to learn which herbs are better suited to hot or cold infusions and which herbs work best for decoctions.

Once they are ready, you can use your infusions and decoctions as a base for many other herbal remedies. They can be used as douches, enemas, herbal baths, fomentations, and steam inhalations amongst many others. Water based herbal preparations are usually the preferred method for extracting mucilaginous herbs, as opposed to tinctures which are alcohol based. There are some plants which are more soluble in alcohol such as hemp and myrrh, which are used in tinctures instead.

Here are some pros and cons of making decoctions:

Pros

Creating a decoction is one of the best ways to draw medicine out of dried roots or other tough, woody parts of the herb. Decoction is necessary for this process, as these parts of the herb are tougher and won't release all their beneficial properties by simply being soaked in boiling water. Decoctions are more potent than teas; in fact, they are some of the most potent out of all herbal preparations. They are absorbed quickly by our bodies, so they work faster and more effectively than some other herbal remedies.

Cons

Decoctions are very potent. They are very concentrated as they have been simmered; hence they have a very strong and intense flavor. People who have delicate digestive systems or are picky eaters with sensitive palates might have a hard time drinking this.

Important Things to Note While Making Infusions, Teas, and Decoctions

Before making any herbal infusions, decoctions, or teas, you need to keep the following things in mind.

Not all herbs are medicinal; neither should they be used for making medicinal remedies. While preparing your mixtures, you can't just leave the pot uncovered. If you don't cover the pot while you're boiling or simmering or steeping your mixture, all the aromatic oils in the herbs will escape into the air. This will make your concoction lose its potency. A simple solution to this would be to simply cover the pot with a lid, which will cause the steam emitting from your mixture to condense back into the water.

There is a reason why using aluminum or metallic pots is not recommended while making infusions, teas, and decoctions. Metals like aluminum, tin, and iron tend to leach into the tea, infusing them with a metallic taste and metallic properties which can be hazardous to our health. It is better to use pots made from glass or ceramic instead. On some occasions, you can get away with using stainless steel or copper pots, but make sure you scour them thoroughly before use, scraping away any impurities and washing it clean. As a good rule, it is best to wash all of your utensils before using. Even if you are using glass, ceramic, enameled pots, or clay pottery, make sure it is not chipped and totally clean.

Never make your infusions or decoctions in unfiltered, tap water. You must use pure water to make sure you're not unwittingly adding any impurities to your mix. Impure water can contain microbes or dirt which can ruin your infusion or decoction. The best thing to do would be to use distilled water or fresh, spring water.

When preparing your infusion make sure you boil the water first, then remove it from the heat and pour the water over the herb. For both decoctions and infusions, strain the steeped tea entirely before sealing your container with a lid and storing it in a cool and dark place, or the fridge. Even though you should ideally consume your infusions and decoctions as soon as they are cool enough to drink, you can store them in the fridge for up to a day or two.

Juicing

Sometimes the best way to extract nutrients from an herb is by juicing the fresh herb. There are specific herbs such as spring picked nettles or wheat grass that are especially nutritious once juiced. You can use different juicers to combine herbs with different vegetables, such as carrots and celery, for the maximum nutritional value. You can also add herbs in a blender with fruit juices, to enhance flavor. However, when mixing fruit juice in herbs, you need to be careful as oxidation can occur quite quickly. To prevent this from happening, you should strain the liquid before you drink it. If you own a food processing machine, you can also press the herbs to extract its juice.

Fomentation

Fomentation is a process more commonly known as a compress. Fomentations basically use herbal infusions or decoctions and apply them in a topical form. You can prepare both hot and cold fomentations, depending mainly upon the herb which is being prepared. Hot and cold fomentations both serve different purposes.

Hot fomentations are used to relax tight and constrained muscles and to promote blood flow throughout the skin by stimulating vasodilation. This helps especially when you have sore muscles and aching legs, and it can also help alleviate internal congestion.

Cold fomentation can restrict blood vessels in the skin. This is helpful for treating acute burns, nasty bruises, or other inflammations in the skin. Fomentations are great natural remedies for the skin and are generally used to treat ailments like eczema, psoriasis, and skin rashes.

Fomentation is created by taking a decoction or an infusion and multiplying its potency by fourfold. Then the mixture is dipped in a natural fabric such as cotton, silk, or wool. After soaking in the mixture, the excess liquid is wrung out of the fabric, and the wet cloth is draped over the affected area. You can also put a dry towel or cloth over the fomentation to retain its temperature, and wrap some plastic cling-film around it to prevent the liquid from dripping all over the place.

Poultice

A poultice is basically a mixture of herbs and water. It is kind of like a paste which is applied to wounded skin. To create a poultice, you select your herbs then macerate them and put them over the wound to have a soothing effect. It can be as straightforward as ripping up some yarrow leaves and placing them on top of cut skin, or chewing some plantain leaves until they are soft and squishy and rubbing them over a bee sting.

There are other ways to make poultices as well. You can spread the herbal mixture on a white cloth and apply the mixture to the wound on the skin.

You can also cover the herbal coating with plastic wrap to prevent the nutrients from escaping. You can add flaxseed or cornmeal to any herbal poultice to hold it in place and act as a base. You just have to grind up some flaxseed, or take some ground cornmeal and mix it in with the powdered herb. Apply it to the wound and change it every three to seven hours. The ground up flaxseed or cornmeal makes a sticky mass that holds the poultice in place. The flaxseed can also be warmed up to make a warm poultice to promote healing.

Oils

There are various types of oils that can be prepared as herbal remedies.

Infused Oils

These are oils infused with herbs, meant to form a protective covering on the skin. They are always applied topically with the intention of soothing cracked and dry skin, and to heal basic irritations, muscle pain, and inflammations. Even though oils get absorbed by the skin much faster than salves or creams, it is not a good idea to use oils on open wounds. You can, however, use infused oils on burns depending on the severity of the burn and how healed it is.

Herbal infused oils can also be especially prepared to be consumed. These oils are prepared with a specific technique and used in cooking to enrich the flavor of a dish, while also adding health benefits from the cooking herb that is used.

You can always find pure vegetable oils at the supermarket. You're probably used to cooking with oils such as sunflower, olive oil, or almond oil. They work well with medicinal herbs as they can easily dissolve the active, fat-soluble actions of these herbs. This is the process of infusion and how these oils are made.

Do remember that there is a vast difference between herbal infused oils and essential oils, and the parameters for using both are entirely different.

Essential Oils

Essential oils are created from the volatile, oily parts of aromatic herbs, trees, and grasses. These oils are extracted from tiny glands that can be found within the leaves, roots, flowers, resins, and wood of these herbs.

There are four main methods that can be used to extract essential oils. You can extract them using steam distillation, solvent extraction, effleurage, and expression.

When using steam distillation, the oil is extracted from the herb by working it with hot steam. Then the herb is selectively condensed with water from which it is separated. When you are using expression to extract essential oil, the oil is extracted through the process of centrifugation or by exerting pressure on the herb.

Solvent extraction is carried out by dissolving the oil in a volatile solvent that leaves a heavy, naturally waxy substance called concrete once the solvent is evaporated. When the mixture is separated from the concrete, the liquid remaining is called an absolute. The absolute is the most concentrated form of the scent available, making it a potent essential oil.

Getting essential oil through effleurage is the longest process. You need to dissolve the oils in animal fat, then separate them using alcohol. Essential oils can be used in cosmetics and for aromatherapy; different essential oils have different therapeutic and healing properties. Essential oils are never used internally.

Preparing Herbal Oils

There are various ways you can prepare herbal oils for your remedies. One of the easiest and most beneficial oils to use is extra virgin, cold-pressed olive oil. This is because it has a lot of nutrients and does not go rancid at room temperature for a very long time. You can also opt for cold-pressed grape-seed oil, almond oil, or apricot oil. These are exceptionally beneficial for facial products for cosmetic use.

While preparing herbal oils, you can use fresh or dried herbs, but make sure there is no excess moisture in your herbal mixture. If you are using fresh herbs, you can wilt them on purpose by setting them in a warm and dry place to get rid of all the moisture.

Once you have your herbs, place them in a mason jar or any non metal container. Coat the herbs in oil, adding at least two to three inches and tightly close the lid. It is ideal to keep adding an inch of oil after some intervals to avoid bacteria spoiling the oil.

Ointments and Salves

Making ointments and salves become a relatively easy process after you've mastered making oils. Herbal salves are made by incorporating infused herbal oil in beeswax, along with other types of topical butter, such as cocoa butter or shea butter, based on their nourishing qualities on the skin. Beeswax is the preferential base; beeswax is thick, and salves tend to be thicker in consistency than ointments and creams. The thicker consistency is helpful because the salve can stay on the skin for a longer time. This makes them more capable of deeply penetrating the muscles and the tissues, acting more effectively.

You can make salves by decocting herbs in oils and then straining the herb out. After the herbs are strained, just add beeswax to the oil and let it cool. You can apply salves as healing ointments on the skin and also on dry and chapped lips as lip balm.

You can keep salves for several months if they are kept in tightly sealed containers in a cool and dark place. If you see any mold or signs of spoilage, toss it out immediately.

Ointments are similar to salves. After you separate the simmered herbs from the liquid, you get a solid mixture of wax or fat that carries the medicinal constituents of the herbs. You can also use petroleum jelly or paraffin wax for your ointment if you're looking for a thinner ointment with a jelly-like consistency.

Tinctures and Liniments

You can use any part of the herb to create a tincture. Tinctures use alcohol or apple cider vinegar to extract the herb's healing properties instead of water. A tincture is far more concentrated than an infusion and also takes a longer time to prepare. However, since tinctures are created with an alcohol base, you can store them for a longer time, for up to a couple of years.

Tinctures are often more effective than infusions because alcohol draws out the herb's medicinal properties more successfully than water. However, these properties vary from herb to herb. For example, as mentioned above, raspberry leaves and nettles work better with water than alcohol, so doing your research before starting is a must.

Tinctures are not hard to make as most medicinal herbs have volatile components that are soluble in alcohol. When you submerge dried or fresh herbs in alcohol, you can easily extract the active agents from the herb in larger concentrations than you ever could with water. These richly concentrated solutions can last for up to two years and are very easy to use medicinally.

Tinctures should ideally be made using pure ethyl alcohol. This type of alcohol is usually distilled from cereals. Problem is, this type of alcohol is not readily available to the public. A good replacement is vodka, with an alcohol content that is at least 35-45 percent. The extraction process doesn't take long; you just need to keep equal parts of herbs and alcohol in a tightly sealed jar. It will hold your mixture until your tincture is ready to be used.

There is a folk method for making tinctures as well where you can use a ratio of 1:2 fresh herbs to alcohol or 1:5 for dried herbs and roots. Make sure you use alcohol with at least 40 percent alcohol content. You can consider using brandy, everclear grain alcohol, or vodka. People who have gluten allergies or suffer from celiac disease will benefit from using vodka and brandy in their tincture.

You should never use any unknown spirit to make tinctures. Also avoid using methyl alcohol, isopropyl alcohol, or methylated spirits. Stick to the alcohol mentioned here and you would have a successful tincture.

Macerations

This is the easiest method of herbal preparation. All you have to do is cover your fresh or dried herbs in cool water and let it soak overnight. In the morning, strain the herb out to separate the liquid. This method is usually used for extremely tender or very fresh herbs, or those herbs that have delicate chemicals that can be destroyed in the heating process, or degraded by high strength alcohol. It is easiest to adapt macerations to modern western methods of medication. Macerations can be turned into tablets or capsules or you can stir the powder from the ground up herbs into smoothies, juice, or water.

Syrups

Syrups are usually made by cooking a jam made out of herbal berries or creating a strong herbal decoction out of the flowers, bark, needles, or leaves of a herb and adding glycerin, honey, or sugar to the mix. People have been creating herbal syrups and cordials for ages to heal sore throats, colds, and coughs and mucus related respiratory conditions. A syrup is a way to make bitter and pungent herbs more appetizing, so that children and picky eaters have an easier time with the remedy.

Syrups are usually used when honey alone cannot do the job and is a good option for vegans who do not eat honey. You can also add unrefined cane sugar or peppermint in syrups to enhance the taste. These are some of the best tasting herbal remedies available but should be taken sparsely because of their sweetness.

Powders and Capsules

This is also a fairly easy way of creating an herbal remedy. You can generally buy a lot of herbs which are already in powder form. You can also powder any herbs you want by yourself in a small coffee grinder, or a small chopper. A capsule blender or chopper will do the job.

If you decide to grind your own herbs, do it carefully and make sure you're sifting any large pieces out of the mix before using.

Powders are very highly concentrated so you don't need to take a large amount, especially when you are consuming the powder orally. An easy way is to put the powder in a capsule to make it easy to take.

You can take loose herbal powder in many different forms, basically depending on what you want it to do for you and which method of taking the powder is most palatable for you. For example, if you are taking herbal powder to reduce imbalances in your body, you can mix it in a medium like applesauce to make it easier to take than just mixing it in with water. Certain people find some herbs to be irritating in the throat or the intestine, so taking powders directly might not be the best idea for them.

You can also encapsulate powdered herbs to make it easier to take. You can use a capsule machine to make capsules. You have the option to use gelatin based capsules or plant based capsules if you are vegan or vegetarian. Capsules take longer to act than powders but are a better way of consuming the entire herb.

You can take most capsules with water or warm herbal tea. If you use cayenne in your capsules, make sure you don't use them with a warm liquid because they can burn in the back of your throat.

You can also use pastilles, which are rolled herbal pills, a traditional method of herbal preparation. Herbal pills are made by mixing powdered herbs with dates or honey and rolling the mixture into small, pill shapes. You can then dehydrate or refrigerate the pills and take them whenever needed.

Pills, Lozenges, and Suppositories

Pills, lozenges, and suppositories are all made in similar ways. You first need to powder your herbs of choice, and then add them to a liquid till they form a stiff dough. You can then shape the mixture as required.

If you're making pills or lozenges, you can use powdered herbs that have proven benefits for coughs and colds with water and honey to make a paste. You can add a couple of drops of essential oil, such as peppermint or wintergreen oil, for the added benefits and a pleasant aroma. You can make the mixture thicker by adding herbs like comfrey root, slippery elm, or marshmallow root powder. This will help give your mixture dough like consistency.

Once you have your dough, pinch off a small amount from the dough ball to make a pill or a lozenge. A lozenge is slightly bigger than a pill in size. Roll the dough into a small ball and flatten it by pressing it between your fingers. You can then cover it with carob powder or more slippery elm. Then put your pills or lozenges into a very low heated oven, or you can also set them out in the sun for a day. Once they are dried out they will last you a long time.

Suppositories are a good way to deliver herbs right into the vagina or the rectum. They are generally used in pill form. They might seem messy once they dissolve and whatever is left behind leaks out; they still tend to be easier to use and less annoying than enemas or douches.

Many people opt for suppositories in lieu of douches for vaginal infections, as the pressure from the douche infusion can actually shove the infection further up the cervix. Suppositories are also a better way to deliver herbs that are more resinous, which do not extract like they are supposed to in water based remedies.

You can make a suppository by mixing powdered herb in melted cocoa butter. This is an easy and convenient way to deliver the herbs directly into the vagina or the rectum. Some suppositories are even used for nasal passages.

Baths and Bathing Remedies

Herbal baths are one of the oldest forms of plant-based healing techniques. These have been used for over thousands of years in different ways, in different parts of the world. Herbal baths are both safe and effective, meant to be relaxing and soothing as the user allows the healing properties of herbs to permeate through the skin.

There are many different ways of taking herbal baths. The Amazons popularized vapor baths, as herbs with menthol are added to water as you soak up the healing properties. Herbal baths are also run by tying specific dried herbs in cheesecloth and hanging the bundle over the tap as the water runs into the bath. You can also pre-prepare a potent infusion and pour it into your bathwater.

The temperature of the bath also plays a vital role in healing. A warm bath helps relax fatigued muscles while a cool bath refreshes and stimulates the body. You should never bath in water hotter than 98 degrees as you run the risk of dehydrating the skin. Very hot baths can also be exhausting. If you're taking a cool bath, the water should be between 70-85 degrees in order to be refreshing and invigorating.

Herbal bathing remedies have been the same for thousands of years and have even been incorporated into modern medicine. The skin can absorb chemicals seeping out from the herbs, which can diffuse into the fat tissue under the skin and go in our blood stream.

Fresh herbs are preferred to be used in some bathing remedies. They are chopped or crushed beforehand and then added to the bath water. If you don't have fresh herbs, you can try making a decoction or a super strong infusion with dried herbs and pouring the mixture in your bathwater. Bathing remedies should be practiced for at least 15 to twenty minutes.

Here are some herbs, classified by type, that you can use in your bathing remedies:

- **Stimulating herbs:** basil, bay, calendula flowers, citronella, fennel, lavender flowers, lemon verbena, lovage roots, mint, rosemary, sage, savory, thyme
- **Soothing herbs:** catnip, chamomile flowers, comfrey, elder, evening primrose flowers, hyssop, jasmine flowers, juniper berries, lemon balm, mullein, passionflower, rose flowers, slippery elm, vervain, violet
- **Tonic herbs:** blackberry leaves, comfrey, dandelion, ginseng root, jasmine flowers, nettle, orange, patchouli, raspberry leaves

- **Herbs for muscles and joints:** agrimony, bay, juniper berries, mugwort, oregano, sage
- **Antiseptic herbs:** yellow dock, eucalyptus, sandalwood
- **Astringent herbs:** agrimony, bay, bayberry, clary, comfrey, dock, frankincense, lady's mantle, lemongrass, mullein, nasturtium flowers, raspberry leaves, rose flowers, rosemary, white willow bark, witch hazel, yarrow

Now that you know various methods of herbal preparations, here are some tools that you need beforehand, so the preparation process is easy for you.

Essential Tools Every Herbalist Needs

As a budding herbalist, you would need the following tools in order to easily make any herbal preparations:

Scissors and Baskets

The very first thing you need is a pair of sharp scissors to cut your herbs with and a basket to carry your herbs in. You can find the baskets cheaply at thrift stores. When you're buying scissors, make sure they are good quality, with a fine blade, so you can cut through tough stems and roots without facing any problems.

Fine Mesh Sieve in Different Sizes

Fine mesh sieves are very useful for straining the herbs from the liquid. Different sized sieves are ideal for different mixtures of herbs. Sometimes if herbs are finely chopped or you are using the delicate, leafy parts for infusions, you would need a small sieve with fine wiring. Ideally, owning three different sizes of sieves will suffice for your infusions, tinctures, oils, and other herbal preparations.

Potato Ricer

Buying a potato ricer is a life hack for pressing herbs. Herb pressers and hydraulic presses are so expensive, so to successfully squeeze out all the tincture and oil from your herbs, a potato ricer is the best choice. It gets every last bit of liquid out of your herbs, so it is very effective and easy to use.

Mortar and Pestle

If you want to lightly bruise herbs to let out their acting agents, or grind them into a consistency of your choice, a mortar and pestle are good tools to carry out this function. Not only are they aesthetically pleasing, they work well to grind herbs in amounts too small to use in the mechanical grinder.

Spice Grinder

You can use a handheld or electric grinder to grind different combinations of herbs together. You can also use it to grind up your dried herbs. You can also put herbs in manual pepper grinders to grind small quantities of herbs.

Kitchen Scale

A kitchen scale is absolutely necessary while you're making herbal preparations because you have to get the herbal measurements just right to avoid overdosing. This helps you control the potency of your remedies as well.

Stainless Steel Funnel

This is essential when you want to transfer your herbal infusions after straining into mason jars or containers. The funnel can be made from plastic too, but stainless steel is best to avoid impurities.

Tea Strainer

These are useful when creating herbal infusions as teas. A tea strainer keeps the aromatic volatile oils in your herbal tea contained until you are ready to drink the tea, so you get the ultimate experience with full taste and flavor. Stainless steel strainers with lids are a good option to buy.

Electric Kettle

Many people consider this item a luxury rather than an essential but it makes boiling water for brewing teas for infusions fairly easy. There is less chance of spilling and accidents and you can make several cups at the same time. However, it is up to you if you decide to purchase this or not.

Now that you have all the tools that you need for your herbal preparations, you have to make sure that you use them safely to avoid any unfortunate mishaps.

You now know how to make your herbal preparations, but where do you source your herbs from in the first place?

Chapter 6: Sourcing Herbs

There are many different ways you can obtain herbs to use in your home remedies. You have the option of getting fresh herbs, which you can either grow or buy, or getting dried herbs which are readily available at the store. You also have the option to buy seeds so you can grow these herbs yourself, or buy or make essential oils and flower essences, depending on how you want to use them.

This chapter will explain how you can source and store different herbs to use in your herbal home remedies.

How to Source Fresh Herbs

The best way to get fresh herbs is to grow your own. However, because of climate and location, this might not always be possible. It is ideal if you have a garden to grow herbs; there are some herbs that you can grow indoors as well, but your options will be limited.

You can buy fresh herbs from the farmers' market or online, but they are usually expensive and spoil easily. Most garden variety herbs are not difficult to grow but growing some medicinal herbs can be a little complicated. You can grow your own basic herbs by following the steps given:

Step One: Decide Which Herb to Grow

You can grow certain herbs in a sunny spot in your garden, or you can even plant them indoors in a pot where sunlight streams through your window. Some of the easiest herbs to grow include basil, mint, chives, tarragon, and rosemary.

- **Growing basil:** If you decide to grow basil, you would need to sow it frequently to make sure you always have a fresh supply. It is one of the best herbs to grow as your first plant because it is so versatile. All it needs is some well-drained soil and good old sunshine.
- **Growing chives:** Chives are a great garnish and can grow easily in your garden. Growing chives can also help repel insects from your garden.
- **Grow mint:** Mint is the best herb for a newbie to grow as it is hardy and difficult to

mess up. You can grow mint in damp, fertile soil in a partially shady or sunny area. Mint is a great garnish and can be added to drinks for flavor.

Step Two: Do You Want Fast or Slow Growing Herbs?

Herbs grow in different cycles. Ask yourself if you want an annual, perennial or biennial herb. Annual and biennial herbs include coriander, dill, parsley, and dill. They grow fast and you might need to sow them at regular intervals through spring and summer so you always have a supply. Perennial herbs include thyme, mint, sage, oregano, rosemary, and chives. They take a longer time to grow so it is best to grow them in a garden.

Step Three: Grow a Cutting or Buy Seeds

If you're ambitious, you can buy seeds and try to grow your herbs from scratch, or you can buy potted plants which are already growing. You can also grow many herbs from small cuttings from a mature herb. You can get the seeds and saplings from any nursery. If you want to use a cutting to grow your first herb, consider mint because it is the easiest.

Step Four: Do Your Research!

You have to make sure you put in a good amount of time researching the individual requirements of the herbs you decide to grow. You need to figure out how much and how frequently they need to be watered, how much light it needs, and what is the optimal temperature for growth. Some herbs also have specific needs in terms of the texture and humidity of the soil and its pH level.

Step Five: Water it Right!

Make sure you know exactly how much water a plant needs to grow successfully. You cannot overwater or under-water a plant. This is the main reason why your herbs can fail. You can always let the top of the soil dry out between your watering sessions, but don't let the soil become completely dry. Make it a routine and you will become attuned to your plants' needs.

Step Six: Take Care While Harvesting

When harvesting your herbs make sure to cut back to a leaf or a step. This looks better than leaving stubs and also is healthier for the plant and will let it heal faster. Cutting the tip off the stem will enable new growth of leaves along the nodes of the plant because the hormones of the plant are distributed this way.

Step Seven: Increase Production

You can make your plant more productive by splitting it. You can also grow a cutting to increase production.

If you want to use parts of the herb faster than they are growing, you can always split the plant if it has multiple stems, or you can dip a cutting of the plant into a rooting hormone and plant it to produce more plants. This is a great way to grow more herbs without spending money on a new plant.

You can follow these steps to grow basic herbs in your garden and your home. You can also research online to figure out ways to grow specific herbs. Once you have the tools, the actual growing is not that complicated.

However, if you feel like you don't have a green thumb, you can always buy your herbs online or at the farmer's market.

How to Source Dried Herbs

Dried herbs are available readily in most supermarkets and whole food stores. You can also get good deals on dried herbs online. You can also dry your own herbs by baking them in the over or setting them out in the sun.

If you don't grow a specific herb in your own garden, you can order them by the pound from various websites. You can research and find which websites are local to you to get the best deals. You can order in small batches at first to check the quality. Make sure they are freshly harvested and properly dried, and you would be able to get superior qualities of dried herbs.

If you cannot find good quality dried herbs online, you can check local farms in your area. Some of these farms also sell their dried herbs online. If it is a hard-to-find herb, you can also check national listings to see what the shipping process is like and make your order accordingly.

How to Obtain Herb Seeds

There are many online nurseries that sell organic herb seeds. You can do some research to see which local nurseries in your area have an online presence. If you don't mind going out and doing some physical shopping, there is nothing better than going to local farms and nurseries and selecting seeds by hand.

You can start by ordering small batches of seeds and seeing which ones result in the most successful germination. Some websites also sell books and guides on how to grow specific herbs from seeds and use them as plant based medicine, so be sure to check those out.

There are also many seed companies that sell out of shops or stalls at the farmers market. You can also buy seeds from garden stores and co-ops as well as online.

You can also try trading seeds with like minded local gardeners. A good practice to adopt is also saving seeds from your own garden whenever you can for more options.

How to Obtain Herbal Plants/Starts

You can purchase organic herbal plants or starts from local growers. You can check out gardens in your area to get pollinator plant starts to grow your herbs and you will discover that you can get hundreds of different varieties of herbs. Some gardens and nurseries offer mail order plants so you won't even have to leave your home to get them. You can call ahead and see what options these places have for selling or check out their online catalogue.

There are many local farms that grow organic produce that sell herbs and vegetables starts at the beginning of spring all the way to early summer. There are a few that sell their starts both online or onsite at their farm and at the farmers market as well.

You can check out your local chain of co-ops to see what kind of organic herbs and vegetable starts they sell as well. It would be a good idea to ask them about their pest management skills beforehand though.

You can recycle these plant starts by cutting parts off the plants you buy to grow more in your own garden.

How to Get Herbal Tinctures

This book has previously explained in detail how you can make your own herbal tinctures at home. You can also buy herbal tinctures from local pharmacies and herbal stores. You can also do some research to see which ones sell these tinctures at a discount.

However, if you have the herbs for it, there is no reason why you should spend any extra money on herbal tinctures when you can just make them yourself, according to your needs.

How to Get Flower Essences

Flower essences are used in aromatherapy and to get energetic reactions similar to homeopathy. Flower essences work more on the emotions than on the body. They are made with a plant infusion which is placed in sunlight directly. After some time, certain parts of the herbs are separated and the remaining liquid essence is preserved mixed with brandy. They are that easy to make at home.

However, many shops sell flower essences if you don't have the time to make them yourself. You can find them at the local herbalist/apothecary as well as online.

How to Obtain Essential Oils

Essential oils are the easiest to buy as they are readily available in a lot of different places. The trick is to find good quality essential oils. There are many fake essential oils that are synthetically made and available cheaply. The best thing to do would be to make your own; how to do so is mentioned in a previous chapter. You can buy essential oils from local stores as they make them in smaller batches so usually put more time and effort into their oils. If you're buying from a big brand, make sure they are legitimate so you get the best quality for your cash.

Chapter 7: Herbal Remedies

So far in the book, you have read a lot about herbal remedies that you can make at home by learning the different healing properties of herbs. However, there is no reason to make your own remedies for a lot of different problems, as there are many preexisting remedies that have existed for centuries, and have been effectively healing people over the ages.

A Guide to Herbal Remedies

Herbal remedies are simply using plants as medicine. We use them to heal; to prevent getting sick and to cure diseases. Herbal remedies can help us feel more energized, they can help ease our symptoms, and even help us lose weight or relax. However, it is essential to use these remedies smartly and safely:

Herbal Treatments Are NOT Medicine Substitutes

Please do not use herbals as replacements for modern medicine. Herbals are aids that are meant to facilitate the work done by allopathic medicine, they are not meant to replace them entirely.

Herbal medicines are rarely regulated or tested before being sold, so they might not always work as claimed. Some herbals carry misleading labels, so you need to be very sure before putting something in your body.

How to Be Safe When Using Herbal Treatments

Make sure you are safe and informed when you're consuming herbal remedies. Always read the product descriptions if you're buying the remedy and don't fall for miracle cures and products that promise the world; they won't always deliver.

Always keep in mind anecdotal evidence is not scientific proof. Some products are sold using testimonials and real-life stories. Your friend could swear by a certain remedy, but just because it worked for someone else, doesn't mean it will work on you.

Discuss your options with a healthcare professional before consuming anything and do not give supplements to children or the elderly. Avoid using herbals if you're pregnant or breastfeeding unless you're taking something specifically approved for that purpose (Medline Plus, 2018).

Herbal Remedies Using Common Herbs and Spices

You'd be amazed to discover that you can make many herbal remedies from the herbs and spices you already have in your kitchen and pantry. Here are some herbal remedies you can make using common herbs and spices:

CARDAMOM

Cardamom
Cardamom can be used in various herbal remedies. You can add powdered cardamom in tea to soothe a sore throat; you can chew

cardamom to enhance oral health and boil cardamom in water and drink it for improved kidney health.

Cinnamon

Cinnamon can help you lose weight. Add ¼ tsp of cinnamon powder with 1 tsp of honey in a cup of hot water and drink it on an empty stomach to melt belly fat. Having ½ tsp of cinnamon powder a day also improves heart health.

Black Pepper

Black pepper improves digestion, adding it to soups can clear congestion, and you can even add pepper to your laundry to prevent the color from fading from your clothes.

Cumin

Cumin is used to clear skin infections such as pimples and boils. Make a paste with cumin powder and vinegar and apply it to your face for clear skin. Including cumin in daily meals prevents anemia and massaging with cumin oil or drinking cumin water reduces anxiety.

A Guide to Common Medicinal Herbs

The following herbs can be commonly found in any household and are known to carry medicinal properties:

Ginger

Ginger can cure symptoms such as upset stomach, cold sweats, and dizziness, which are commonly experienced during flu season. You can suck on raw ginger root as a cough suppressant or if that is too extreme, steep ginger in hot water to make herbal tea for sore throats.

Thyme

Brew thyme in combination with other herbs such as mint to relieve congestion. You can inhale thyme with other aromatic herbs to breathe better and relieve congestion.

Turmeric

Turmeric carries amazing anti-inflammatory properties. If you drink a glass of turmeric milk daily, you can boost your immunity and also be strong enough to fight the flu virus.

Mint

You can use mint or peppermint to open up your nasal passages and help you breathe through a stuffy nose. The fragrance of the mint can be released through steam, which you can inhale to let the menthol in the leaves unclog your nasal passages.

Herbal Remedies for a Range of Ailments and Afflictions

Here is a list of herbal remedies to treat a variety of ailments:

- **Abscesses:** Mix 1 tsp turmeric powder with milk or water and apply directly on abscess.
- **Gingivitis:** Add three drops of tea-tree oil to water and use as mouthwash.
- **Acne:** Apply apple cider vinegar on a cotton ball on the affected area.
- **Aging:** Boil 4 teaspoons of honey with 1 tsp of cinnamon in 3 cups of water. Drink the tea daily.
- **Allergies:** Mix nettle leaf with raspberry leaves to make a tea to soothe allergy symptoms.
- **Anemia:** Juice beetroot and apples together and drink daily.
- **Asthma:** Mix garlic powder with milk and drink at the first sign of an asthma attack.
- **Back Pain:** Mix eucalyptus essential oil with a carrier oil and massage onto the back.
- **Bedsores:** Rub aloe vera on the sores to soothe the inflamed skin.
- **Bites and Stings:** A poultice from fresh plantain leaves works immediately.
- **Burns and Sunburns:** Aloe vera works wonders for burns. You can also apply chickweed paste.
- **Cold Sores:** Apply a dab of tea-tree oil on a cotton swab and put on the sore.
- **Constipation:** Dandelion tea can help relieve constipation.
- **Cramps:** Cramping can be calmed by drinking chamomile tea.
- **Fever:** Add 1 teaspoon of basil powder with ¼ tsp of black pepper in hot water with honey and drink.
- **Snoring:** Apply a dab of peppermint oil on the nose to stop snoring.
- **Insomnia:** Add some lavender oil in a diffuser and let the scent permeate the air to cure insomnia.

Conclusion

Health and wellness are tricky to manage in our lives. We have so many options for healthcare and wellness these days that we end up being confused about what we want in our lives and what is the best way for us to feel healthy and well.

The trick is to remember the way of the Native Americans. They believe in a simple approach; heal all the parts of the body to heal the body as a whole. Be close to nature, treat yourself well. Don't ignore your mental and spiritual health. Let love in and take care of yourself. Practice moderation and live a balanced life.

Only then can one be truly healthy.

This book is not meant to replace allopathic medicine. In fact, the herbal remedies and recipes provided here are just to facilitate you on your journey toward healing. You can do these herbal remedies in combination with your pre-existing medical treatments, with the advice of a healthcare professional.

If you do not have any existing medical conditions, then you have more freedom to explore the wellness aspect of the *Native American Herbal Apothecary*.

Apply the principles of Sacred Medicine to your life, create your own herbal remedies, and live your best life.

Be true to yourself, that is the only way you can be close to the universe, and do justice to the life that has been bestowed upon you.

Good luck!

References

A guide to herbal remedies Information | Mount Sinai - New York. (n.d.). Mount Sinai Health System. Retrieved May 10, 2021, from https://www.mountsinai.org/health-library/special-topic/a-guide-to-herbal-remedies

A guide to herbal remedies: MedlinePlus Medical Encyclopedia. (2018). Medlineplus.gov. https://medlineplus.gov/ency/patientinstructions/000868.htm

A Look at the History of Herbs. (n.d.). UniversalClass.com. Retrieved May 10, 2021, from https://www.universalclass.com/articles/health/herbs/alternative-medicine/a-look-at-the-history-of-herbs.htm#:~:text=A%20Look%20at%20the%20History%20of%20Herbs.%20Herbs

All That's Interesting. (2015, October 31). The Historical Origins Of The Witch. All That's Interesting; All That's Interesting. https://allthatsinteresting.com/history-of-witches

Alvarado, D. M. (2017, September 12). Herbal Mojo: The Use of Herbs in Healing and Magick. HubPages. https://discover.hubpages.com/health/Rootwork-The-Healing-and-Magickal-Power-of-Herbs-Plants-and-Roots

Anonymous. (2019, November 3). Herbal remedies for all diseases. A Good Fit. https://www.weightcf.com/2019/11/herbal-remedies-for-all-diseases.html

Augur, D. (n.d.). Herbal Preparations. Herbs and Natural Remedies for Health. http://herbsandnaturalremedies.com/herbal-preparations/

Borchers, A. T., Keen, C. L., Stern, J. S., & Gershwin, M. E. (2000). Inflammation and Native American medicine: the role of botanicals. The American Journal of Clinical Nutrition, 72(2), 339–347. https://doi.org/10.1093/ajcn/72.2.339

Bulgin Graham, A.-M. (2015, September 26). Herbal Preparations | Medicinal Herbs - Medicinalherbs-4u.com. Www.medicinalherbs-4u.com. https://www.medicinalherbs-4u.com/herbal-preparations.html

by. (2015, July 31). How to Understand and Make a Sacred Medicine Wheel ⋆ LonerWolf. LonerWolf. https://lonerwolf.com/medicine-wheel/

Dana. (2019, September 5). 10 Essential Tools Every Herbalist Needs. Rustic Farm Life. https://www.rusticfarmlife.com/essential-tools-every-herbalist-needs/

Esposito, M. L., & Kahn-John, M. (2020). How Should Allopathic Physicians Respond to Native American Patients Hesitant About Allopathic Medicine? AMA Journal of Ethics, 22(10), 837–844. https://doi.org/10.1001/amajethics.2020.837.

Food desk, N. (2017, November 6). Flu Season: Keep These Herbs and Spices Handy to Protect Yourself. NDTV.com. https://www.ndtv.com/food/flu-season-keep-these-herbs-and-spices-handy-to-protect-yourself-1771688

Four Herbs that Act as Natural Birth Control. (2014, June 12). Top 10 Home Remedies. https://www.top10homeremedies.com/news-facts/four-herbs-act-natural-birth-control.html#:~:text=Another%20herb%20that%20is%20used%20as%20a%20natural

Garilli, B., Sather, R., & Foley, M. A. (2014). A Guide to Common Medicinal Herbs - Health Encyclopedia - University of Rochester Medical Center. Rochester.edu. https://www.urmc.rochester.edu/encyclopedia/content.aspx?contenttypeid=1&contentid=1169

H.S. (2020, January 11). The Four Sacred Medicines. Ojibwe Journal. https://ojibwejournal.wordpress.com/2020/01/11/the-four-sacred-medicines/

Healing Plants - Medicine Ways: Traditional Healers and Healing - Healing Ways - Exhibition - Native Voices. (2019). Nih.gov. https://www.nlm.nih.gov/nativevoices/exhibition/healing-ways/medicine-ways/healing-plants.html

Hema, Dr. (2017, February 9). 20 Home Remedies with Spices from your Kitchen. My Little Moppet. https://www.mylittlemoppet.com/home-remedies-with-spices/

Hill, A. (2020, February 3). 9 Popular Herbal Medicines: Benefits and Uses. Healthline. https://www.healthline.com/nutrition/herbal-medicine#2.-Ginseng

History of Opium. (n.d.). Opium.com. https://opium.com/history/

https://www.facebook.com/Drugscom. (2019). Quinine. Drugs.com; Drugs.com. https://www.drugs.com/mtm/quinine.html

Jeanroy, A. (2021, January 7). Where to Buy Fresh Herbs Online. The Spruce. https://www.thespruce.com/where-to-buy-herb-plants-online-1761730#:~:text=Where%20to%20Buy%20Fresh%20Herbs%20Online%201%20Richters.

Jones, S., & Jones, E. (2012, April 3). A-Z Herb Use. Www.ancient-Wisdom.com. http://www.ancient-wisdom.com/herbsaz.htm

Kukreja, K. (2014, December 2). Top 10 Home Remedies To Treat Abscess. STYLECRAZE. https://www.stylecraze.com/articles/home-remedies-to-treat-abscess/

Leech, J. (2017, June 4). 10 Delicious Herbs and Spices With Powerful Health Benefits. Healthline. https://www.healthline.com/nutrition/10-healthy-herbs-and-spices#TOC_TITLE_HDR_2

Lovern, L. L., & Locust, C. (2013). Native American Beliefs Concerning Health and Unwellness. Native American Communities on Health and Disability, 77–93. https://doi.org/10.1057/9781137312020_5

Maslowski, D. (2013, November 15). Old Remedies Your Grandma Used That You Can Too. DIY Natural. https://www.diynatural.com/old-remedies-that-still-work/

Mason, M. (2015, January 7). How To Source Quality Herbs. Growing up Herbal. https://growingupherbal.com/source-quality-herbs/

Native American Medicine. (n.d.). Health and Fitness History. Retrieved May 10, 2021, from https://healthandfitnesshistory.com/ancient-medicine/native-american-medicine-health/#:~:text=The%20practice%20of%20Native%20American%20medicine%20goes%20back

Osuch, J. (2013, January 26). Food Storage: Storing Herbs and Spices for Long Term Storage. Seed to Pantry School. https://seedtopantryschool.com/food-storage-storing-herbs-and-spices-for-long-term-storage/#:~:text=The%20very%20best%20way%20to%20obtain%20the%20freshest

ParksNov. 5, C., 2004, & Am, 10:00. (2004, November 5). Ancestors of Science: Native American Medicine. Science | AAAS. https://www.sciencemag.org/careers/2004/11/ancestors-science-native-american-medicine

Pitt, C. (2015, October 27). The truth in traditional medicine. BBC News. https://www.bbc.com/news/health-34616695

poofpantry. (2016, January 19). Fresh Herbs vs Dried Herbs. The Poof Pantry. https://poofpantry.wordpress.com/2016/01/19/fresh-vs-dried-herbs/

Pozzi, K. (2013, December 27). Different Kinds Of Herbal Preparations Explained. Www.herbgeek.com. http://www.herbgeek.com/different-kinds-of-herbal-preparations-explained/

Ramey, Dr. D. (2018, February 17). The Curious History of Herbs and Plants as Medicines. David Ramey, DVM. https://www.doctorramey.com/herbs-and-plants-history/

Rankin, L. (n.d.-a). Introducing Sacred Medicine. Lissa Rankin. Retrieved May 10, 2021, from https://lissarankin.com/introducing-sacred-medicine/

Rankin, L. (n.d.-b). Sacred Medicine: 21 Things About Healing They Didn't Teach Me In Medical School. Lissa Rankin. Retrieved May 10, 2021, from https://lissarankin.com/sacred-medicine-21-things-about-healing-they-didnt-teach-me-in-medical-school/

Report, S. (Ed.). (2019, April 21). 50 plants mentioned in the Holy Quran at Islamic garden. Gulfnews.com. https://gulfnews.com/uae/50-plants-mentioned-in-the-holy-quran-at-islamic-garden-1.63465305

Roberts, N. F. (2020, November 29). 7 Native American Inventions That Revolutionized Medicine And Public Health. Forbes. https://www.forbes.com/sites/nicolefisher/2020/11/29/7-native-american-inventions-that-revolutionized-medicine-and-public-health/?sh=3693e0161e73

Saba, H. (2018, September 5). How To Choose The Best Herbal Preparation For Your Needs. Herbal Academy. https://theherbalacademy.com/choose-best-herbal-preparation/

Sacred Pipe | Find Your Power. (2019, December 26). Www.findyourpowersd.com. https://www.findyourpowersd.com/our-traditions/sacred-pipe/

sarah. (2017, May 31). A Glimpse into the Intuitive Medicine of the Native American Tradition. Www.ancient-Origins.net. https://www.ancient-origins.net/history-ancient-traditions/glimpse-intuitive-medicine-native-american-tradition-008157

Smith, C. (2017, January 10). Native American History: A Tale of Medicine. The Differential. http://www.thedifferentialdx.com/native-american-history-a-tale-of-medicine/

soulhealer. (2018, August 14). Medicinal Herbs: A Guide To Herbal Preparation Methods. Medical Intuitive - Psychic Readings - Energy Healing. https://medical-intuitives.com/medicinal-herbs-herbal-preparation-methods/

Standish, L. (n.d.). Sacred Medicines. Sacred Medicines. Retrieved May 10, 2021, from https://www.sacredmedicines.earth/

Stewart, E. (2017, November 28). How to Source High Quality Herbs, Essential Oils, & Herbal Products + Where I Buy Mine. Aroma Culture. https://www.aromaculture.com/blog/where-to-buy-herbs-and-essential-oils

Sturluson, T. (n.d.). Medicinal Herbs Guide. The Herbal Resource. Retrieved May 10, 2021, from https://www.herbal-supplement-resource.com/

The Four Sacred Medicines – Indigenous Website. (n.d.). Northern College Indigenous Council. http://www.northernc.on.ca/indigenous/four-sacred-medicines/

Top 10 Herbs and Spices to Boost Your Brainpower. (2013, November 25). Top 10 Home Remedies. https://www.top10homeremedies.com/kitchen-ingredients/top-10-spices-boost-brainpower.html

Turner, N. J. (2019, May 1). Indigenous Peoples' Medicine in Canada | The Canadian Encyclopedia. Thecanadianencyclopedia.ca. https://www.thecanadianencyclopedia.ca/en/article/native-medicines

Vemireddy, R. (2020). The Role of Native American Healing Traditions Within Allopathic Medicine. Inquiries Journal, 12(12). http://www.inquiriesjournal.com/articles/1849/the-role-of-native-american-healing-traditions-within-allopathic-medicine

Visser, M. (2017, December 26). 14 Must-Have Supplies For Herbalists (Plus A Free Printable Supply List). Herbal Academy. https://theherbalacademy.com/supplies-for-herbalists/

W. Brown, J. (n.d.). Native American Contributions to Science, Engineering and Medicine. https://science.sciencemag.org/content/sci/189/4196/38.full.pdf

WAY, D. (2015, March 27). Herbal preparation methods. Herbalism. https://dspermaculture.wordpress.com/2015/03/27/herbal-preparation/#:~:text=Herbal%20preparation%20methods%201%20Infusion.%20This%20is%20often

Weiser, K. (2019). Native American Medicine – Legends of America. Legendsofamerica.com. https://www.legendsofamerica.com/na-medicine/

Winter, C. (2020, October 21). Infusion, Decoction, or Tincture? Which Herbal Preparations to Use for Different Plant Parts. MorningChores. https://morningchores.com/herbal-preparations/]

acs.org (n.d.). Albert Szent-Gyorgyi Vitamin C - Landmark. American Chemical Society. Retrieved August 14, 2021, from https://www.acs.org/content/acs/en/education/whatischemistry/landmarks/szentgyorgyi.html#:~:text=The%20existence%20of%20vitamin%20C%20was%20long%20suspected.

ag.ndsu.edu (n.d.). The Thistles of North Dakota — Publications. Www.ag.ndsu.edu. Retrieved August 6, 2021, from https://www.ag.ndsu.edu/publications/crops/the-thistles-of-north-dakota#section-2

altnature.com (n.d.). Lobelia Herb Uses - Learn about Herbs. Altnature.com. Retrieved August 3, 2021, from https://altnature.com/gallery/lobelia.htm#:~:text=Lobelia%20was%20used%20as%20a%20Ceremonial%20%28Emetic%29%20

Amy (2020, May 22). Medicinal Uses for Yarrow—The Homestead Herb | Amy K. Fewell. Amy K Fewell | the Fewell Homestead. https://thefewellhomestead.com/medicinal-uses-for-yarrow-the-homestead-herb/

Anderson, K (2017, March 23). The Original Medicinal Plant Gatherers & Conservationists. United Plant Savers. https://unitedplantsavers.org/the-original-medicinal-plant-gatherers-conservationists/

Anderson, T (1996, July). Conservation Native American Style. PERC. https://www.perc.org/1996/07/01/conservation-native-american-style/

Andriote, J.-M (2012, November 6). The Mysterious Past and Present of Witch Hazel. The Atlantic. https://www.theatlantic.com/health/archive/2012/11/the-mysterious-past-and-present-of-witch-hazel/264553/

Ann, G (2012, December 14). Chicory Weed. Wikinut. https://www.wikinut.com/guides/gardening/chicory-weed/

Aseem Malhotra (2018, August 30). Why modern medicine is a major threat to public health | Aseem Malhotra. The Guardian; The Guardian. https://www.theguardian.com/society/2018/aug/30/modern-medicine-major-threat-public-health

Avant, J. T (2020, September 11). North America Known As Turtle Island To Indigenous Tribes. CapeNews.net. https://www.capenews.net/mashpee/columns/north-america-known-as-turtle-island-to-indigenous-tribes/article_450f4f21-6782-52c3-8c43-34c928a81b40.html

Bantilan, C (2019, October 24). What Is Oregon Grape? Uses and Side Effects. Healthline. https://www.healthline.com/nutrition/oregon-grape#other-uses

Barhum, L (n.d.). Benefits and Side Effects of Bloodroot. Verywell Health. Retrieved August 9, 2021, from https://www.verywellhealth.com/bloodroot-4175168#:~:text=Possible%20Side%20Effects%20Bloodroot%20is%20generally%20safe%20when

Baumgardner, D. J (2016). Stinging Nettle: the Bad, the Good, the Unknown. Journal of Patient-Centered Research and Reviews, 3(1), 48–53. https://doi.org/10.17294/2330-0698.1216

Beattie, O (2006, February 7). Scurvy | The Canadian Encyclopedia. Www.thecanadianencyclopedia.ca. https://www.thecanadianencyclopedia.ca/en/article/scurvy#:~:text=Scurvy%20was%20a%20serious%20problem%20throughout%20the%20whole

bio.brandeis.edu (n.d.). Purple Coneflower (Echinacea purpurea) Species Page. Www.bio.brandeis.edu. Retrieved August 10, 2021, from http://www.bio.brandeis.edu/fieldbio/Wildflowers_Kimonis_Kramer/PAGES/PURPLECONEFLOWER_PAGE_FINAL.html

Blankespoor, J (2016, April 13). Violet's Edible and Medicinal Uses. Chestnut School of Herbal Medicine. https://chestnutherbs.com/violets-edible-and-medicinal-uses/

brainchildnutritionals.com (n.d.). Oregon Grape Root Extract. Brainchild Nutritionals. Retrieved August 11, 2021, from https://www.brainchildnutritionals.com/products/oregon-grape-root-extract-1-oz#:~:text=Herbalists%20count%20on%20Oregon%20Grape%20to%20support%20healthy

Brennan, K (2020, September 9). lobelia for lung congestion, asthma, anxiety and more. TruFoods Nutrition. https://trufoodsnutrition.com/lobelia-and-herb-for-asthma-lung-congestion-seizures-anxiety-and-depression/#:~:text=Lobelia

britannica.com (n.d.-a). Eclecticism | philosophy and theology. Encyclopedia Britannica. Retrieved August 16, 2021, from https://www.britannica.com/topic/eclecticism

britannica.com (n.d.-b). Jewel orchid | plant. Encyclopedia Britannica. Retrieved August 4, 2021, from https://www.britannica.com/plant/jewel-orchid

britannica.com (n.d.-c). Yellow lady's slipper | plant. Encyclopedia Britannica. Retrieved August 4, 2021, from https://www.britannica.com/plant/yellow-ladys-slipper

britannica.com (2021, July 25). Mint | plant. Encyclopedia Britannica. https://www.britannica.com/plant/Mentha

Brito, I (2020, August 28). These Are the the Benefits of Slippery Elm for Babies. Mommybites. https://mommybites.com/healthy-living/slippery-elm-benefits-babies/

BrowserMedia (2020). Tribal Nations & the United States: An Introduction | NCAI. Ncai.org. https://www.ncai.org/about-tribes#:~:text=There%20are%20574%20federally%20recognized

cabi.org (n.d.). Achillea millefolium (yarrow). Www.cabi.org. Retrieved August 6, 2021, from https://www.cabi.org/isc/datasheet/2636

Carroll, J (n.d.). StackPath. Www.gardeningknowhow.com. Retrieved August 19, 2021, from https://www.gardeningknowhow.com/edible/herbs/st-johns-wort/st-johns-wort-plant-care.htm

Cassaro, R (2011, December 1). The Ancient "Doctrine of Signatures" Suppressed By The Establishment. Richard Cassaro. https://www.richardcassaro.com/the-ancient-doctrine-of-signatures-suppressed-by-the-elite/#:~:text=The%20Doctrine%20of%20Signatures%20is%20profound%20ancient%20wisdom

Chantlaca (2013, May 3). UNPFIP Network: House of Mica: The Message of the Hopi at the United Nations. UNPFIP Network. https://unpfip.blogspot.com/2013/05/house-of-mica-message-of-hopi-at-united.html

Charlie (2010, September 11). Mormon Tea. http://www.swordofsurvival.com/2010/09/mormon-tea.html

Cherney, K (2019, August 9). Hyssop Oil Uses, Benefits, Side Effects and How to Use it. Healthline. https://www.healthline.com/health/hyssop-oil#precautions

chicproject.eu (2020, February 27). Commercial exploitation of chicory as a multipurpose crop. CHIC Project. http://chicproject.eu/2020/02/27/commercial-exploitation-of-chicory-as-a-multipurpose-crop/

Christiansen, S (2020a). The Health Benefits of Oregon Grape. Verywell Health. https://www.verywellhealth.com/oregon-grape-benefits-4590368

Christiansen, S (2020b, May 8). The Health Benefits of Uva Ursi. Verywell Health. https://www.verywellhealth.com/uva-ursi-health-benefits-4582831

Collins, J (n.d.). The Status of Native American Women: A Study of the Lakota Sioux. https://www.drake.edu/media/departmentsoffices/dussj/2006-2003documents/StatusCollins.pdf

Cooper, G (2016). COYOTE IN NAVAJO RELIGION AND COSMOLOGY. https://academics.lmu.edu/media/lmuacademics/cures/urbanecolab/module12/Coyote%20Mythology%20M12.L1.pdf

D, W (2011). Types of Hawthorn Trees That Produce Edible Berries | eHow.com. EHow.com. https://www.ehow.com/info_7848401_types-trees-produce-edible-berries.html

Davis, J., & Greenfield, J (2006, September 30). Bloodroot (Sanguinaria canadensis L.) | NC State Extension Publications. Content.ces.ncsu.edu. https://content.ces.ncsu.edu/bloodroot-sanguinaria-canadensis-l

Dellwo, A (2020, December 24). The Health Benefits of Yarrow. Verywell Health. https://www.verywellhealth.com/yarrow-health-benefits-4586386

Di Maria, L (2020, March 22). Benefits and Risks of Using St. Johns Wort for Childhood Depression. Verywell Mind. https://www.verywellmind.com/st-johns-wort-for-child-depression-1066682

Dillon, R. D (2021, May 20). Stinging Nettle for Allergies: Benefits and Herbal Remedies. Becca Ink. https://www.beccaink.com/stinging-nettle-for-allergies/

Dodril, T (2019, July 26). How to Identify Chicory • New Life On A Homestead. New Life on a Homestead. https://www.newlifeonahomestead.com/how-to-identify-chicory/#:~:text=The%20ground%20level%20leaves%20on%20chicory%20plants%20are

Dr. Axe (2018, August 2). The Plant Alkaloid that Treats Diabetes & Digestive Problems. Dr. Axe. https://draxe.com/nutrition/berberine/

drhealthbenefits.com (2017, July 13). 17 Scientific Health Benefits of Chicory Coffee. DrHealthBenefits.com. https://drhealthbenefits.com/food-bevarages/beverages/coffee/health-benefits-chicory-coffee#:~:text=17%20Scientific%20Health%20Benefits%20of%20Chicory%20Coffee%20

drstandley.com (2021). Lady's Slipper (Cypripedium pubescens) - Herbs, Herbs A-Z, Herbs Listings, Herbs Resource, Herbs Information. Drstandley.com. https://www.drstandley.com/herbs_ladys_slipper.shtml#:~:text=POTENTIAL%20SIDE%20EFFECTS%3ALady%27s%20slipper%20species%20may%20contain%20volatile

drugs.com (2021, July 21). Chicory Uses, Benefits & Dosage - Drugs.com Herbal Database. Drugs.com. https://www.drugs.com/npp/chicory.html#22263588

eattheplanet.org (2021, January 22). American Wild Mint - Eat The Planet American Wild Mint american herb. Eat the Planet. https://eattheplanet.org/american-herb/

eatweeds.co.uk (2018, April 23). Wild Garlic or Ramsons - A Foraging Guide to Its Food, Medicine and Other Uses. EATWEEDS. https://www.eatweeds.co.uk/wild-garlic-allium-ursinum#:~:text=Some%20people%20are%20allergic%20to

ecampusontario.pressbooks.pub (n.d.). The Medicine Wheel Teachings. Pressbooks.pub. Retrieved July 31, 2021, from https://ecampusontario.pressbooks.pub/movementtowardsreconciliation/chapter/the-medicine-wheel-teachings/

ediblewildfood.com (n.d.-a). Elderberry: Identification, Leaves, Bark & Habitat | Sambucus canadensis. Www.ediblewildfood.com. Retrieved August 6, 2021, from https://www.ediblewildfood.com/elderberry.aspx

ediblewildfood.com (n.d.-b). Wild Violet: Pictures, Flowers, Leaves & Identification | Viola odorata. Www.ediblewildfood.com. Retrieved August 10, 2021, from https://www.ediblewildfood.com/wild-violet.aspx#:~:text=Violet%20leaves%20are%20palmate%2C%20alternate%2C%20and%20are%20somewhat

emedicinehealth.com (n.d.). Mormon Tea: Uses, Side Effects, Dose, Health Benefits, Precautions & Warnings. EMedicineHealth. Retrieved August 7, 2021, from https://www.emedicinehealth.com/mormon_tea/vitamins-supplements.htm

Emily (n.d.). four directions - Traditional Native Healing. Traditionalnativehealing.com. Retrieved August 1, 2021, from https://traditionalnativehealing.com/tag/four-directions

Emily (2015, January 19). four directions - Traditional Native Healing. Traditional Native Healing. https://traditionalnativehealing.com/tag/four-directions

encyclopedia.com (n.d.-a). Chamomile | Encyclopedia.com. Www.encyclopedia.com. Retrieved August 12, 2021, from https://www.encyclopedia.com/plants-and-animals/plants/plants/chamomile#:~:text=This%20native%20of%20southern%20and%20central%20Europe%20is

encyclopedia.com (n.d.-b). Mormon Tea | Encyclopedia.com. Www.encyclopedia.com. Retrieved August 7, 2021, from https://www.encyclopedia.com/sports/sports-fitness-recreation-and-leisure-magazines/mormon-tea

encyclopedia.com (2013). Witch Hazel | Encyclopedia.com. Encyclopedia.com. https://www.encyclopedia.com/plants-and-animals/plants/plants/witch-hazel

FiberandBead.com (2014, November 27). Medicine Men. Native American Shamanism. http://fiberandbead.com/medicine-men/

firstnationspedagogy.ca (2009). Interconnectedness Overview from the First Nations Pedagogy Online Project. Firstnationspedagogy.ca. https://firstnationspedagogy.ca/interconnect.html

firstpeople.us (n.d.). The Eagle's Revenge - A Cherokee Legend. Www.firstpeople.us. Retrieved August 1, 2021, from https://www.firstpeople.us/FP-Html-Legends/TheEaglesRevenge-Cherokee.html

Fletcher, J (2020, January 3). Ginger: Health benefits and dietary tips. Www.medicalnewstoday.com. https://www.medicalnewstoday.com/articles/265990#_noHeaderPrefixedContent

Flowers, J (2013, June 26). "Bloodroot" … War Paint and the Medicine Man. Birds and Blooms. https://birdsandblooms.me/2013/06/26/bloodroot-war-paint-and-the-medicine-man/

Foster, S (n.d.). Hawthorn, Chinese hawthorn, English hawthorn, one-seeded Hawthorn, Crataegus laevigata photos, Crataegus pinnatifida photos, Crataegus monogyna photos, article by Steven Foster. Www.stevenfoster.com. Retrieved August 6, 2021, from https://www.stevenfoster.com/education/monograph/hawthorn.html

fourdirectionswellness.com (2018, August 7). Native American Healing Ceremonies -. Four Directions Wellness. https://fourdirectionswellness.com/2018/08/07/native-american-healing-ceremonies/

fs.fed.us (n.d.). Crataegus douglasii. Www.fs.fed.us. Retrieved August 6, 2021, from https://www.fs.fed.us/database/feis/plants/shrub/cradou/all.html#3

fs.fed.us (2019a). Sambucus racemosa. Fs.fed.us. https://www.fs.fed.us/database/feis/plants/shrub/samrac/all.html

fs.fed.us (2019b). Wild Ginger. Fs.fed.us. https://www.fs.fed.us/wildflowers/plant-of-the-week/asarum_canadense.shtml

G, P (2019, September 3). Native American Religion and Spirituality - Common Threads, Unique Beliefs, and Too Many Misconceptions. PowWows.com - Native American Pow Wows. https://www.powwows.com/native-american-religion-and-spirituality-common-threads-unique-beliefs-and-too-many-misconceptions/

Gadacz, R. R (2019). Sun Dance | The Canadian Encyclopedia. Thecanadianencyclopedia.ca. https://www.thecanadianencyclopedia.ca/en/article/sun-dance

gardenia.net (n.d.). Cichorium intybus (Chicory). Gardenia.net. Retrieved August 4, 2021, from https://www.gardenia.net/plant/cichorium-intybus

gobotany.nativeplanttrust.org (n.d.-a). Lobelia inflata (bladder-pod lobelia, indian-tobacco): Go Botany. Gobotany.nativeplanttrust.org. Retrieved August 5, 2021, from https://gobotany.nativeplanttrust.org/species/lobelia/inflata/

gobotany.nativeplanttrust.org (n.d.-b). Mentha canadensis (American wild mint): Go Botany. Gobotany.nativeplanttrust.org. Retrieved August 9, 2021, from https://gobotany.nativeplanttrust.org/species/mentha/canadensis/

goorchids.northamericanorchidcenter.org (n.d.). Cypripedium acaule (Moccasin Flower, Pink Lady's Slipper): Go Orchids. Goorchids.northamericanorchidcenter.org. Retrieved August 9, 2021, from http://goorchids.northamericanorchidcenter.org/species/cypripedium/acaule/

Government of Canada, N. R. C (n.d.). The M9 Cascadia Megathrust Earthquake of January 26, 1700. Www.earthquakescanada.nrcan.gc.ca. Retrieved August 16, 2021, from https://www.earthquakescanada.nrcan.gc.ca/historic-historique/events/17000126-en.php

Graves, D (2010, May 3). Jacques Cartier Landed in Newfoundland. Christianity.com. https://www.christianity.com/church/church-history/timeline/1501-1600/jacques-cartier-landed-in-newfoundland-11629956.html

Gregutt, P (n.d.). Lobelia | Encyclopedia.com (R. J. Frey, Ed.). Www.encyclopedia.com. Retrieved August 5, 2021, from https://www.encyclopedia.com/plants-and-animals/plants/plants/lobelia

Gupta, M (2018, June 26). Ginger for Babies: Is It Safe, Health Benefits & Safety Measures. Parenting.firstcry.com. https://parenting.firstcry.com/articles/ginger-for-babies-health-benefits-and-safety-measures/

Hallal, F (2021, April 6). Bloodroot: Benefits, Uses, Precautions, and Dosage. Healthline. https://www.healthline.com/nutrition/bloodroot#benefits-risks

Haw, G (2017, July 9). Native Americans used to smoke lobelia as a cure for lung disease. Education Quizzes. https://www.educationquizzes.com/education-matters/2017/07/native-americans-used-to-smoke-lobelia-as-a-cure-for-lung-disease/

healthbenefitstimes.com (2018, January 25). Wild Garlic facts and health benefits. Healthbenefitstimes.com. https://www.healthbenefitstimes.com/wild-garlic/

healthbenefitstimes.com (2020, October 12). Wild Licorice facts and health benefits. Healthbenefitstimes.com. https://www.healthbenefitstimes.com/wild-licorice/

healthyfocus.org (2016, November 7). 7 Proven Echinacea Health Benefits. Healthy Focus. https://healthyfocus.org/echinacea-health-benefits/

herbal-supplement (2014, April 15). Peppermint – Health Benefits and Side Effects. The Herbal Resource. https://www.herbal-supplement-resource.com/peppermint-herb.html

herbco.com (n.d.). Blood root. Monterey Bay Spice Company. Retrieved August 4, 2021, from https://www.herbco.com/c-151-blood-root.aspx#:~:text=Native%20Americans%20used%20the%20underground%20parts%20of%20bloodroot

herbpathy.com (n.d.). Rhus Typhina Herb Uses, Benefits, Cures, Side Effects, Nutrients. Herbpathy. Retrieved August 8, 2021, from https://herbpathy.com/Uses-and-Benefits-of-Rhus-Typhina-Cid4510

herbrally.com (n.d.). Lobelia Monograph. HerbRally. Retrieved August 3, 2021, from https://www.herbrally.com/monographs/lobelia#:~:text=Nineteenth-century%20eclectic%20healers%20and%20herbalists%20were%20sometimes%20called

herbwisdom.com (n.d.). Uva Ursi Benefits & Information (Arctostaphylos Uva-ursi). Herbwisdom. Retrieved August 6, 2021, from https://www.herbwisdom.com/herb-uva-ursi.html

hgic.clemson.edu (n.d.). Wild Ginger. Home & Garden Information Center | Clemson University, South Carolina. Retrieved August 9, 2021, from https://hgic.clemson.edu/factsheet/wild-ginger/

Higuera, V (2020, August 27). Is It Safe to Use Chamomile Tea for Babies? Healthline. https://www.healthline.com/health/baby/chamomile-tea-for-babies#benefits-and-uses

Hitz, B (2019, September 11). North American Sumacs You Should Know About. The Spruce. https://www.thespruce.com/sumac-trees-and-shrubs-3269722

Hobbs, C (n.d.). Echinacea: From Native American Pancea to Modern Phytopharmaceutical. Dr. Christopher Hobbs. Retrieved August 2, 2021, from https://www.christopherhobbs.com/library/articles-on-herbs-and-health/echinacea-from-native-american-pancea-to-modern-phytopharmaceutical/

Hodge, F. W (2019). Medicine Men & Healing Practices – Legends of America. Legendsofamerica.com. https://www.legendsofamerica.com/na-medicineman/

holybasilfarm (2019, July 13). Medicinal Herb Profile: Anise Hyssop. Holy Basil Farm. https://www.holybasil.farm/post/medicinal-herb-profile-anise-hyssop#:~:text=Uses%3A%20Anise%20Hyssop%20has%20been

Hope, N (n.d.). Native American Animals: the Bear (Mato) is a gift to Mother Earth and her people. Blog.nativehope.org. Retrieved August 2, 2021, from https://blog.nativehope.org/native-american-animals-bear-mato-is-a-gift-to-mother-earth-and-her-people

Horne, S (n.d.). Herbal Medicine for Infants and Toddlers. Www.treelite.com. Retrieved August 19, 2021, from https://www.treelite.com/NF/2008/05/Herbal-Medicine-for-Infants-and-Toddlers

Hosseini, A., & Mirazi, N (2014). Acute administration of ginger (Zingiber officinale rhizomes) extract on timed intravenous pentylenetetrazol infusion seizure model in mice. Epilepsy Research, 108(3), 411–419. https://doi.org/10.1016/j.eplepsyres.2014.01.008

httpwarpaths2peacepipes.com (n.d.). Crow Symbol ***. Www.warpaths2peacepipes.com. Retrieved August 2, 2021, from https://www.warpaths2peacepipes.com/native-american-symbols/crow-symbol.htm

huffpost.com (2011, August 14). A Spot Of Tea Could Help ADHD: STUDY. HuffPost. https://www.huffpost.com/entry/tea-adhd_n_925962

illinoiswildflowers.info (n.d.). Witch-Hazel (Hamamelis virginiana). Illinoiswildflowers.info. Retrieved August 6, 2021, from https://illinoiswildflowers.info/trees/plants/witch_hazel.htm

Jackson, D., & Bergeron, K (n.d.). Wild Ginger Herb uses, Dangers and Warnings. Altnature.com. Retrieved August 9, 2021, from https://altnature.com/gallery/wild_ginger.htm

Jerrod (2020, April 8). 25 Sacred Native American Flowers & Native American Wild Rose. Native American Love Forever. https://nativeamericanloveforever.com/native-american-flowers/

Jessop, E (n.d.). Lesson Plan - Corn. Teacherlink.ed.usu.edu. Retrieved July 30, 2021, from http://teacherlink.ed.usu.edu/tlresources/units/Byrnes-celebrations/corn.html

Joe (2019, March 7). Greenbrier – Winter and Spring Wild Edible. Eat the Planet. https://eattheplanet.org/greenbrier-winter-and-spring-wild-edible/

Johorey, J (2013, October 21). 8 Asthma In Children Herbal Remedies, Natural Treatments And Cure | AyurvedicCure.com. Ayurvediccure.com. https://ayurvediccure.com/8-excellent-herbal-remedies-for-asthma-in-children/#:~:text=Another%20culinary%20herb%20which%20can%20also%20be%20used

Joseph, B (2017). A Definition of Smudging. Ictinc.ca. https://www.ictinc.ca/blog/a-definition-of-smudging

Josue, M (2020, September 30). Violet (Viola) Flowers: Types, How to Grow and Care. Florgeous. https://florgeous.com/violet/#:~:text=Violets%20are%20low%20growing%20annuals%20or%20short-lived%20perennials

joybileefarm.com (2019, February 18). Agastache for Herbal Remedies and Culinary Herbs and Use Its Licorice Flavor. Joybilee® Farm | DIY | Herbs | Gardening |. https://joybileefarm.com/agastache-herbal-remedies/#:~:text=It%20is%20safe%20for%20infants%2C%20children%20and%20can

jungledragon.com (n.d.). Roundleaf Greenbrier (Smilax rotundifolia) - JungleDragon. Www.jungledragon.com. Retrieved August 9, 2021, from https://www.jungledragon.com/specie/17650/roundleaf_greenbrier.html#:~:text=%27%27Smilax%20rotundifolia%27%27%2C%20known%20as%20roundleaf%20greenbrier%20and%20common

Kacman, E (n.d.). Chamomile for colds for children: medicinal properties | Competently about health on iLive. Iliveok.com. Retrieved August 12, 2021, from https://iliveok.com/health/how-drink-chamomile-children-cold-and-flu_129226i15828.html

Kent, T. H (n.d.). Smilax rotundifolia (Common greenbrier). Florafinder.org. Retrieved August 9, 2021, from https://florafinder.org/Species/Smilax_rotundifolia.php

Kimbroug, K. A., & Swift, C. E (n.d.). Growing Lavender in Colorado - 7.245. Extension. Retrieved August 5, 2021, from https://extension.colostate.edu/topic-areas/yard-garden/growing-lavender-in-colorado-7-245/

King, R (n.d.). Lobelia. Herballegacy.com. Retrieved August 13, 2021, from https://herballegacy.com/King_Dosages.html#:~:text=

Kneller, J (2021, April 13). 11 powerful medicinal plants Native Americans use to cure everything - Dr. James Kneller MD. Dr. James Kneller. https://jamesknellermd.com/11-medicinal-plants-used-to-cure-everything/#4_Greenbrier

Krueger, S (2019, January 14). Where Did All of These Weeds Come From? Emergence.fbn.com. https://emergence.fbn.com/agronomy/where-did-all-of-these-weeds-come-from#:~:text=Dandelions%20are%20currently%20one%20of%20the%20most%20common

Landschoot, P., Abbey, T., & Delvale, T (2019, June 5). Lawn and Turfgrass Weeds: Wild Violet. Penn State Extension. https://extension.psu.edu/lawn-and-turfgrass-weeds-wild-violet

Lee, B., Sur, B., Yeom, M., Shim, I., Lee, H., & Hahm, D.-H (2012). Effect of Berberine on Depression- and Anxiety-Like Behaviors and Activation of the Noradrenergic System Induced by Development of Morphine Dependence in Rats. The Korean Journal of Physiology & Pharmacology : Official Journal of the Korean Physiological Society and the Korean Society of Pharmacology, 16(6), 379–386. https://doi.org/10.4196/kjpp.2012.16.6.379

legendsofamerica.com (n.d.). Old Time Cures & Remedies – Legends of America. Www.legendsofamerica.com. Retrieved August 13, 2021, from https://www.legendsofamerica.com/we-oldremedies/

legendsofamerica.comxt=If%20the%20child%20grows%20an%20inch%20in%20the,Swallow%20one-half%20spoonful%20every%20ten%20seconds%20until%20gone (2018, June 20). Natural Asthma Remedies: Heal Your Child without Medication. Raising Natural Kids. https://raisingnaturalkids.com/natural-asthma-remedies/

Leland, T (n.d.). Download Limit Exceeded. Citeseerx.ist.psu.edu. Retrieved July 25, 2021, from http://citeseerx.ist.psu.edu/viewdoc/download?doi=10.1.1.567.539&rep=rep1&type=pdf

Lindell, J (2011). Characteristics of a Dandelion | Hunker. Hunker. https://www.hunker.com/13426794/characteristics-of-a-dandelion

Lissienko, K (2018, September 17). Ear Infections. KidsHealth NZ. https://www.kidshealth.org.nz/ear-infections#:~:text=Once%20an%20ear%20infection%20is%20diagnosed%2C%20your%20child

lybrate.com (n.d.). Benefits of DAndelion And Its Side Effects. Lybrate. Retrieved August 5, 2021, from https://www.lybrate.com/topic/benefits-of-dandelion-and-its-side-effects

lybrate.com (2020, August 27). Benefits of Cattail And Its Side Effects. Lybrate. https://www.lybrate.com/topic/benefits-of-cattail-and-its-side-effects#cultivation-of-cattail

Mahr, S (n.d.). Bloodroot, Sanguinaria canadensis. Wisconsin Horticulture. Retrieved August 9, 2021, from https://hort.extension.wisc.edu/articles/bloodroot-sanguinaria-canadensis/

Mandl, E (2018, March 8). Elderberry: Benefits and Dangers. Healthline; Healthline Media. https://www.healthline.com/nutrition/elderberry

Martini, E (2002). Jacques Cartier witnesses a treatment for scurvy. Vesalius: Acta Internationales Historiae Medicinae, 8(1), 2–6. https://pubmed.ncbi.nlm.nih.gov/12422875/

mayoclinic.org (2018). High blood pressure in children - Symptoms and causes. Mayo Clinic; https://www.mayoclinic.org/diseases-conditions/high-blood-pressure-in-children/symptoms-causes/syc-20373440

McCoy, J.-A (2017). Lavender: History, Taxonomy, and Production. Ncsu.edu. https://newcropsorganics.ces.ncsu.edu/herb/lavender-history-taxonomy-and-production/

McKenzie, M (2017, September 1). The Most Intelligent Birds In The World. Wingspan Optics; Wingspan Optics. https://wingspanoptics.com/blogs/field-journal/the-most-intelligent-birds-in-the-world

McMillan, M (n.d.). Passionflower: Uses and Risks. WebMD. Retrieved August 13, 2021, from https://www.webmd.com/vitamins-and-supplements/passionflower-uses-and-risks

medicalhealthguide.com (n.d.). Licorice Medicinal Uses, Health Benefits and Side Effects. Www.medicalhealthguide.com. Retrieved August 13, 2021, from http://www.medicalhealthguide.com/herb/licorice.htm

medicalmedium.com (2015, March 22). Mullein. Www.medicalmedium.com. https://www.medicalmedium.com/blog/mullein#:~:text=Mullein%20oil%20%28mullein%20extract%20in%20an%20olive%20oil

medicinalherbinfo.org (n.d.). Bloodroot «Medicinal Herb Info. Medicinalherbinfo.org. Retrieved August 9, 2021, from http://medicinalherbinfo.org/000Herbs2016/1herbs/bloodroot/

Meleen, M (n.d.). Native American Death Rituals & Funeral Customs. Funeral Guide. Retrieved July 30, 2021, from https://www.funeralguide.co.uk/blog/death-around-world-native-american-beliefs

Miller, E., Swanson, A., Phillips, D., Fletcher, T., Liem, A., & Miller, J (1983). Structure-Activity Studies of the Carcinogenicities in the Mouse and Rat of Some Naturally Occurring and Synthetic Alkenylbenzene Derivatives Related to Safrole and EstragÃ³le1. CANCER RESEARCH, 43, 24–1134. https://cancerres.aacrjournals.org/content/canres/43/3/1124.full.pdf

Minogue, K (2015, August 7). Medicine, Myth and the Lady's Slipper Orchid. Shorelines. https://sercblog.si.edu/medicine-myth-and-the-ladys-slipper-orchid/

missouribotanicalgarden.org (n.d.-a). Rhus typhina - Plant Finder. Www.missouribotanicalgarden.org. Retrieved August 8, 2021, from http://www.missouribotanicalgarden.org/PlantFinder/PlantFinderDetails.aspx?kempercode=c337

missouribotanicalgarden.org (n.d.-b). Witch Hazel. Www.missouribotanicalgarden.org. Retrieved August 6, 2021, from https://www.missouribotanicalgarden.org/gardens-gardening/our-garden/notable-plant-collections/witch-hazel.aspx#:~:text=Bloom%20time%20depends%20heavily%20on%20weather.%20The%20common

mottchildren.org (n.d.-a). licorice | CS Mott Children's Hospital | Michigan Medicine. Www.mottchildren.org. Retrieved August 19, 2021, from https://www.mottchildren.org/health-library/d04424a1

mottchildren.org (n.d.-b). St. John's wort | CS Mott Children's Hospital | Michigan Medicine. Www.mottchildren.org. Retrieved August 18, 2021, from https://www.mottchildren.org/health-library/d04408a1#:~:text=feeding%20a%20baby.-

Multum, C (n.d.). Dandelion Uses, Side Effects & Warnings. Drugs.com. Retrieved August 5, 2021, from https://www.drugs.com/mtm/dandelion.html#:~:text=Get%20emergency%20medical%20help%20if%20you%20have%20signs

Myers, V. R (n.d.). North American Sumacs You Should Know About. The Spruce. Retrieved August 8, 2021, from https://www.thespruce.com/sumac-trees-and-shrubs-3269722

Myss, C (2015). The Great Spirit - Caroline Myss. Caroline Myss. https://www.myss.com/free-resources/world-religions/native-american-spirituality/the-great-spirit/

nationalgeographic (2020, April 27). Native Americans and Freedom of Religion. National Geographic Society. https://www.nationalgeographic.org/article/native-americans-and-freedom-religion/

native-languages.org (n.d.-a). Native American Indian Chicory Medicine, Meaning and Symbolism from the Myths of Many Tribes. Www.native-Languages.org. Retrieved August 4, 2021, from http://www.native-languages.org/legends-chicory.htm

native-languages.org (n.d.-b). Native American Indian Coneflower (Elk Root) Medicine, Meaning and Symbolism from the Myths of Many Tribes. Www.native-Languages.org. Retrieved August 5, 2021, from http://www.native-languages.org/legends-coneflower.htm

native-languages.org (n.d.-c). Native American Indian Dandelion Medicine, Meaning and Symbolism from the Myths of Many Tribes. Www.native-Languages.org. Retrieved August 5, 2021, from http://www.native-languages.org/legends-dandelion.htm

native-languages.org (n.d.-d). Native American Indian Lavender Medicine, Meaning and Symbolism from the Myths of Many Tribes. Www.native-Languages.org. Retrieved August 4, 2021, from http://www.native-languages.org/legends-lavender.htm

native-languages.org (n.d.-e). Native American Indian Stinging Nettle Medicine, Meaning and Symbolism from the Myths of Many Tribes. Www.native-Languages.org. Retrieved August 13, 2021, from http://www.native-languages.org/legends-nettle.htm#:~:text=

native-languages.org (n.d.-f). Native American Indian Violet Medicine, Meaning and Symbolism from the Myths of Many Tribes. Www.native-Languages.org. Retrieved August 10, 2021, from http://www.native-languages.org/legends-violet.htm

native-languages.org (n.d.-g). Native American Indian Yarrow Medicine, Meaning and Symbolism from the Myths of Many Tribes. Www.native-Languages.org. Retrieved August 6, 2021, from http://www.native-languages.org/legends-yarrow.htm

nativeamericancultureblog (2016, January 14). Native American Culture & Flowers. Nativeamericancultureblog. https://nativeamericancultureblog.wordpress.com/2016/01/14/native-american-culture-flowers/

nativeamericanherbalism.com (n.d.). Lavender Uses and Healing Properties. Native American Herbalism. Retrieved August 2, 2021, from https://nativeamericanherbalism.com/cosmetic/lavender-uses-healing-properties/

naturalmedicinalherbs.net (n.d.-a). medicinal herbs: AMERICAN LIQUORICE - Glycyrrhiza lepidota. Naturalmedicinalherbs.net. Retrieved August 13, 2021, from http://naturalmedicinalherbs.net/herbs/g/glycyrrhiza-lepidota=american-liquorice.php#:~:text=

naturalmedicinalherbs.net (n.d.-b). medicinal herbs: WAVY-LEAVED THISTLE - Cirsium undulatum. Www.naturalmedicinalherbs.net. Retrieved August 6, 2021, from http://www.naturalmedicinalherbs.net/herbs/c/cirsium-undulatum=wavy-leaved-thistle.php#:~:text=Medicinal%20use%20of%20Wavy-Leaved%20Thistle%3A%20A%20decoction%20of

nccih.nih.gov (n.d.). Echinacea. NCCIH. Retrieved August 5, 2021, from https://www.nccih.nih.gov/health/echinacea

ncnativeethnobotany.org (n.d.). Cattails. NCNative. Retrieved August 7, 2021, from https://www.ncnativeethnobotany.org/cattails

Nemeth, E., & Bernath, J (2008). Biological Activities of Yarrow Species (Achillea spp.). Current Pharmaceutical Design, 14(29), 3151–3167. https://doi.org/10.2174/138161208786404281

Neverman, L (2012, May 23). Weekly Weeder #22 - Wild Geranium + Wildcrafting Wednesday. Common Sense Home. https://commonsensehome.com/wild-geranium/

newsroom.idconsortium.com (2020, February 27). Commercial exploitation of chicory as a multipurpose crop. Commercial Exploitation of Chicory as a Multipurpose Crop. https://newsroom.idconsortium.com/commercial-exploitation-of-chicory-as-a-multipurpose-crop/

Nicoll, R., & Henein, M. Y (2009). Ginger (Zingiber officinale Roscoe): A hot remedy for cardiovascular disease? International Journal of Cardiology, 131(3), 408–409. https://doi.org/10.1016/j.ijcard.2007.07.107

nih.gov (n.d.). "If You Knew the Conditions..." Health Care to Native Americans: United States 19th-Century Doctors Thoughts about Native American Medicine. Www.nlm.nih.gov. Retrieved July 25, 2021, from https://www.nlm.nih.gov/exhibition/if_you_knew/ifyouknew_04.html

northernc.on.ca (n.d.). The Four Sacred Medicines – Indigenous Website. Http://Www.northernc.on.ca/. Retrieved July 26, 2021, from http://www.northernc.on.ca/indigenous/four-sacred-medicines/

nrcs.usda.gov (n.d.). TRADITIONAL SOCIAL STRUCTURES. https://www.nrcs.usda.gov/Internet/FSE_DOCUMENTS/nrcs141p2_023458.pdf

nutrineat.com (2010, May 5). Chicory Root Side Effects - Consume it With Great Precaution. Nutrineat. https://nutrineat.com/chicory-root-side-effects

onlinelibrary.wiley.com (2016, May 26). Lobelia | Encyclopedia.com. Www.encyclopedia.com. https://www.encyclopedia.com/plants-and-animals/plants/plants/lobelia

ozarkedgewildflowers.com (n.d.). Bloodroot (Sanguinaria Canadensis) | ozarkedgewildflowers.com. Retrieved August 9, 2021, from https://ozarkedgewildflowers.com/bloodroot-sanguinaria-canadensis/

P, R (2020a, June 11). Violet Flower Meaning and Symbolism. Florgeous. https://florgeous.com/violet-flower-meaning/#:~:text=In%20Native%20American%20tradition%2C%20there%20is%20a%20Haudenosaunee

P, R (2020b, August 9). Hawthorn Tree Flower Meaning and Symbolism. Florgeous. https://florgeous.com/hawthorn-tree-flower-meaning/#:~:text=Hawthorn%20trees%20and%20flowers%20are%20often%20viewed%20as

Panoff, L (2019, August 29). Ginger for Nausea: Effectiveness, Safety, and Uses. Healthline. https://www.healthline.com/nutrition/ginger-for-nausea#preparations

parentinghealthybabies.com (2016, July 15). Health Benefits of Sage for Children. Parenting Healthy Babies. https://parentinghealthybabies.com/health-benefits-of-sage-for-children/#:~:text=Soothes%20nervous%20and%20excitable%20children%3A%20Sage%20also%20soothes

Parker, L (2011, February 16). Peyote in Native American Traditions. Indigenous Religious Traditions. https://sites.coloradocollege.edu/indigenoustraditions/6-%E2%80%A2-independent-projects/peyote-in-native-american-traditions/

Patterson, S (2014, June 9). 5 Native American Survival Medicines Secretly Made At Home. Off the Grid News. https://www.offthegridnews.com/alternative-health/5-native-american-survival-medicines-secretly-made-at-home/

Perez, J (n.d.). Food as MedicineStinging Nettle (Urtica dioica, Urticaceae) - American Botanical Council. Www.herbalgram.org. Retrieved August 19, 2021, from https://www.herbalgram.org/resources/herbalegram/volumes/volume-15/number-7-july/food-as-medicine-stinging-nettle-urtica-dioica-urticaceae/food-as-medicine/

pfaf.org (n.d.-a). Cirsium undulatum Wavy-Leaved Thistle, Tracy's thistle PFAF Plant Database. Pfaf.org. Retrieved August 6, 2021, from https://pfaf.org/User/Plant.aspx?LatinName=Cirsium+undulatum#:~:text=Physical%20Characteristics%20Cirsium%20undulatum%20is%20a%20PERENNIAL%20growing

187

pfaf.org (n.d.-b). Geranium maculatum Spotted Cranesbill, Spotted geranium, Crowfoot, Wild Geranium, Cranesbill PFAF Plant Database. Pfaf.org. Retrieved August 19, 2021, from https://pfaf.org/user/Plant.aspx?LatinName=Geranium+maculatum

pfaf.org (n.d.-c). Lobelia inflata Indian Tobacco PFAF Plant Database. Pfaf.org. Retrieved August 17, 2021, from https://pfaf.org/user/Plant.aspx?LatinName=Lobelia+inflata

Pharmapproach (2020, July 16). 15 Astonishing Statistics and Facts about U.S. Pharmaceutical Industry. Pharmapproach.com. https://www.pharmapproach.com/15-astonishing-statistics-and-facts-about-u-s-pharmaceutical-industry/#:~:text=The%20U.S.%20represents%20the%20biggest%20market%20for%20pharmaceutical%20products%20in%20the%20world.

Pietrangelo, A (2017, July 31). The Effects of Caffeine on Your Body. Healthline. https://www.healthline.com/health/caffeine-effects-on-body#:~:text=The%20Effects%20of%20Caffeine%20on%20Your%20Body%201

Pietrangelo, A (2018, June 7). St. John's Wort: The Benefits and the Dangers. Healthline. https://www.healthline.com/health-news/is-st-johns-wort-safe-080615#The-benefits-of-St.-Johns-wort

plainshumanities.unl.edu (2011). Encyclopedia of the Great Plains | SWEAT LODGE. Unl.edu. http://plainshumanities.unl.edu/encyclopedia/doc/egp.rel.047

plants.ces.ncsu.edu (n.d.-a). Cypripedium acaule (Moccasin-flower, Pink Lady Slipper) | North Carolina Extension Gardener Plant Toolbox. Plants.ces.ncsu.edu. Retrieved August 9, 2021, from https://plants.ces.ncsu.edu/plants/cypripedium-acaule/

plants.ces.ncsu.edu (n.d.-b). Taraxacum officinale (Dandelion, Lion's Tooth) | North Carolina Extension Gardener Plant Toolbox. Plants.ces.ncsu.edu. Retrieved August 17, 2021, from https://plants.ces.ncsu.edu/plants/taraxacum-officinale/

poncatribe-ne.org (n.d.). Native Foods. Ponca Tribe of Nebraska. Retrieved August 2, 2021, from https://www.poncatribe-ne.org/services/health-services/diabetes-program/native-foods/

primidi.com (n.d.). What are mentha canadensis? | Technology Trends. Www.primidi.com. Retrieved August 8, 2021, from https://www.primidi.com/what_are_mentha_canadensis

Rey-Vizgirdas, E (n.d.). Common Yarrow. Www.fs.fed.us. Retrieved August 6, 2021, from https://www.fs.fed.us/wildflowers/plant-of-the-week/achillea_millefolium.shtml#:~:text=Yarrow%20has%20a%20circumboreal%20distribution.%20It%20is%20found

Richards, L (2020, May 11). Ginger for colds: How to use ginger for a sore throat. Www.medicalnewstoday.com. https://www.medicalnewstoday.com/articles/ginger-for-colds#is-it-effective

rueremedies.com (2019, November 13). 23 Natural Home Remedies For Dermatitis Symptom Relief. TrueRemedies – All True Home Remedies for Better Health. https://trueremedies.com/home-remedies-for-dermatitis/

rxlist.com (n.d.-a). Asarum: Health Benefits, Side Effects, Uses, Dose & Precautions. RxList. Retrieved August 9, 2021, from https://www.rxlist.com/asarum/supplements.htm#SideEffects

rxlist.com (n.d.-b). Oregon Grape: Health Benefits, Side Effects, Uses, Dose & Precautions. RxList. Retrieved August 18, 2021, from https://www.rxlist.com/oregon_grape/supplements.htm

Rybak, C., & Decker-Fitts, A (2009). Understanding Native American healing practices. Counselling Psychology Quarterly, 22(3), 333–342. https://doi.org/10.1080/09515070903270900

Saeedi, M., Morteza-Semnani, K., & Ghoreishi, M-R (2003, September) (PDF) The treatment of atopic dermatitis with licorice gel. ResearchGate. https://www.researchgate.net/publication/9068483_The_treatment_of_atopic_dermatitis_with_licorice_gel

sagecreationsfarm.com (n.d.). Lavender. Sage Creations Organic Farm. Retrieved August 4, 2021, from https://sagecreationsfarm.com/blooms/lavender/

sandmountainherbs.com (n.d.). Medicinal Uses of Agastache foeniculum, Anise Hyssop. Www.sandmountainherbs.com. Retrieved August 18, 2021, from http://www.sandmountainherbs.com/articles/Agastache-foeniculum-medicinal-uses.html

Schilling, V (2014, October 28). Our Brothers and Sisters: 5 Sacred Animals and What They Mean in Native Cultures. Indian Country Today. https://indiancountrytoday.com/archive/our-brothers-and-sisters-5-sacred-animals-and-what-they-mean-in-native-cultures

Schneider, A. A (2016, April 20). How to use nettles for seasonal allergies. SchneiderPeeps. https://www.schneiderpeeps.com/use-nettles-for-seasonal-allergies/#:~:text=

sciencedirect.com (2014). Asarum - an overview | ScienceDirect Topics. Www.sciencedirect.com. https://www.sciencedirect.com/topics/agricultural-and-biological-sciences/asarum

Singh, O., Khanam, Z., Misra, N., & Srivastava, M (2011). Chamomile (Matricaria chamomilla L.): An overview. Pharmacognosy Reviews, 5(9), 82. https://doi.org/10.4103/0973-7847.79103

sittingowl.com (n.d.). Mitakuye Oyasin - All Our Relations. Sittingowl.com. Retrieved August 16, 2021, from http://sittingowl.com/mitakuye_oyasin.htm

skaclothing.co.za (n.d.). What is the difference between a Spirit Animal, a Totem Animal and an animal "Familiar"? What is a Totem Pole? - SKA Clothing. Https://Skaclothing.co.za. Retrieved August 2, 2021, from https://skaclothing.co.za/what-is-the-difference-between-a-spirit-animal-a-totem-animal-and-an-animal-familiar-what-is-a-totem-pole/

slipperorchids.info (2020, June 2). Cribb: Cyp Taxonomy. Www.slipperorchids.info. http://www.slipperorchids.info/taxonomy/cribbcyp.html

snaplant.com (2015, April 10). What is Chicory? History And Uses. Snaplant.com. http://snaplant.com/herbs/what-is-chicory-history-and-uses/#:~:text=Chicory%20was%20cultivated%20as%20early

spiceography.com (2019, August 16). Echinacea: A Native American Cure-All. SPICEography. https://www.spiceography.com/echinacea/#:~:text=Echinacea%20is%20native%20to%20North%20America%20and%20was

splitrockenvironmental.ca (2013). Black Hawthorn (k'an). Splitrockenvironmental.ca. http://splitrockenvironmental.ca/product/black-hawthorn/

St. Joseph's Indian School (2017). Four Directions in Native American Culture | St. Joseph's Indian School. St. Joseph's Indian School. https://www.stjo.org/native-american-culture/native-american-beliefs/four-directions/

Stag's Horn Sumach Rhus typhina (n.d.). Naturalmedicinalherbs.net. Retrieved August 8, 2021, from http://naturalmedicinalherbs.net/herbs/r/rhus-typhina=stag's-horn-sumach.php

Stanton, K. M (2021, January 13). Alligator Symbolism, Meaning & The Alligator Spirit Animal. UniGuide. https://www.uniguide.com/alligator-symbolism-meaning-spirit-animal/#Native_American_Alligator_Meanings

stevenfoster.com (n.d.). Slippery Elm, Ulmus rubra, Ulmus fulva photos and article by Steven Foster. Stevenfoster.com. Retrieved August 12, 2021, from https://stevenfoster.com/education/monograph/Ulmus_rubra.html

Strauch, B (1995, December 1). Herb to Know: Wild Ginger. Motherearthliving.com. https://www.motherearthliving.com/gardening/plant-profile/AN-HERB-TO-KNOW-WILD-GINGER/

Streit, L (2020, May 8). What Is Lobelia, and How Is It Used? Healthline. https://www.healthline.com/nutrition/lobelia#bottom-line

study.com (2020). The Iroquois Creation Story: Summary & Analysis - Video & Lesson Transcript | Study.com. Study.com. https://study.com/academy/lesson/the-iroquois-creation-story-summary-analysis.html

Summers, D (n.d.). Sacred Herbs - Native American. Bellaonline.com. Retrieved July 25, 2021, from http://www.bellaonline.com/articles/art49834.asp

Taylor, J. A., Weber, W., Standish, L., Quinn, H., Goesling, J., McGann, M., & Calabrese, C (2003). Efficacy and Safety of Echinacea in Treating Upper Respiratory Tract Infections in Children. JAMA, 290(21), 2824. https://doi.org/10.1001/jama.290.21.2824

temperate.theferns.info (n.d.). Cirsium undulatum - Useful Temperate Plants. Temperate.theferns.info. Retrieved August 6, 2021, from https://temperate.theferns.info/plant/Cirsium+undulatum

texasbeyondhistory.net (n.d.). Morman Tea. Texasbeyondhistory.net. Retrieved August 7, 2021, from https://texasbeyondhistory.net/ethnobot/images/mormontea.html

The Editors of Encyclopedia Britannica (2018a). Sun Dance | religious ceremony. In Encyclopædia Britannica. https://www.britannica.com/topic/Sun-Dance

The Editors of Encyclopedia Britannica (2018b). cattail | Description, Uses, & Facts. In Encyclopædia Britannica. https://www.britannica.com/plant/cattail

The Survival Mom (2019, April 1). 10 Ways to Use Wild Violets for Food and Medicine. Thesurvivalmom.com. https://thesurvivalmom.com/enjoy-wild-violets/

thecanadianencyclopedia.ca (2017). Sweat Lodge | The Canadian Encyclopedia. Thecanadianencyclopedia.ca. https://www.thecanadianencyclopedia.ca/en/article/sweat-lodge

thefreedictionary.com (n.d.). Green Corn Dance. TheFreeDictionary.com. Retrieved July 30, 2021, from https://encyclopedia2.thefreedictionary.com/Green+Corn+Dance

theherbalacademy.com (2014, April 29). The Virtues of Violets: Health Benefits of Violets. Herbal Academy. https://theherbalacademy.com/health-benefits-of-violets/

toddcaldecott.com (n.d.). Lobelia. Todd Caldecott. Retrieved August 5, 2021, from https://toddcaldecott.com/herbs/lobelia/

treeandlandscapecompany.com (2021, May 5). Wild Mint (Mentha arvensis) - Featured Native Plant of the Week. Tree & Landscape Company. https://www.treeandlandscapecompany.com/native-plant-of-the-week/wild-mint-mentha-arvensis-featured-native-plant-of-the-week/

u-s-history.com (2019). Ghost Dance. U-s-History.com. https://www.u-s-history.com/pages/h3775.html

usgs.gov (n.d.). Cattail (Typha) invasion in North American wetlands. Www.usgs.gov. Retrieved August 7, 2021, from https://www.usgs.gov/center-news/cattail-typha-invasion-north-american-wetlands?qt-news_science_products=3#qt-news_science_products

utahindians.org (n.d.). Early Peoples: The Navajo. Utahindians.org. Retrieved July 29, 2021, from https://utahindians.org/archives/navajo/earlyPeoples.html

Uzoma, K (n.d.). Does Ginger Treat Bloating? LIVESTRONG.COM. Retrieved August 18, 2021, from https://www.livestrong.com/article/522902-does-ginger-treat-bloating/

Verdiell, Z (2020, February 22). Where does chicory grow? Askinglot.com. https://askinglot.com/where-does-chicory-grow#:~:text=Chicory%2C%20also%20known%20as%20succory%2C%20blue-sailors%20and%20ragged-sailors%2C

Vilímovský, M (2015, June 10). Benefits and side effects of lavender tea. Medlicker.com. https://medlicker.com/882-lavender-tea-benefits-side-effects#:~:text=Side%20effects%20of%20lavender%20tea%201%20Breast%20growth

virtualmuseum.ca (n.d.). The Healing Power of Plants - Past Remedies. Www.virtualmuseum.ca. Retrieved August 12, 2021, from http://www.virtualmuseum.ca/sgc-cms/expositions-exhibitions/plantes-plants/pastremedies.php

vlegendsofamerica.com (n.d.). Herbs, Plants, and Healing Properties – Page 9 – Legends of America. Www.legendsofamerica.com. Retrieved August 13, 2021, from https://www.legendsofamerica.com/na-herbs/9/#Wild%20Garlic

Wahl, R. A., Aldous, M. B., Worden, K. A., & Grant, K. L (2008). Echinacea purpurea and osteopathic manipulative treatment in children with recurrent otitis media: a randomized controlled trial. BMC Complementary and Alternative Medicine, 8(1). https://doi.org/10.1186/1472-6882-8-56

warpaths2peacepipes.com (n.d.-a). Meaning of Animals ***. Www.warpaths2peacepipes.com. Retrieved August 11, 2021, from https://www.warpaths2peacepipes.com/native-american-culture/meaning-of-animals.htm

warpaths2peacepipes.com (n.d.-b). Turtle Symbol ***. Www.warpaths2peacepipes.com. Retrieved August 2, 2021, from https://www.warpaths2peacepipes.com/native-american-symbols/turtle-symbol.htm

warpaths2peacepipes.com (2012, November 20). Bear Symbol ***. Warpaths2peacepipes.com. https://www.warpaths2peacepipes.com/native-american-symbols/bear-symbol.htm

WebMD (2009). Ginger: Uses, Side Effects, Interactions, Dosage, and Warning. Webmd.com. https://www.webmd.com/vitamins/ai/ingredientmono-961/ginger

WebMD (2019). Slideshow: Health Benefits of Ginger. WebMD. https://www.webmd.com/diet/ss/slideshow-health-benefits-ginger

webmd.com (n.d.-a). Passionflower: Uses, Side Effects, Interactions, Dosage, and Warning. Www.webmd.com. Retrieved August 19, 2021, from https://www.webmd.com/vitamins/ai/ingredientmono-871/passionflower

webmd.com (n.d.-b). Passionflower: Uses, Side Effects, Interactions, Dosage, and Warning. Www.webmd.com. Retrieved August 21, 2021, from https://www.webmd.com/vitamins/ai/ingredientmono-871/passionflower

webmd.com (n.d.-c). SAGE: Overview, Uses, Side Effects, Precautions, Interactions, Dosing and Reviews. Www.webmd.com. Retrieved August 19, 2021, from https://www.webmd.com/vitamins/ai/ingredientmono-504/sage#:~:text=Some%20species%20of%20sage%2C%20such

webmd.com (n.d.-d). WORMWOOD: Overview, Uses, Side Effects, Precautions, Interactions, Dosing and Reviews. Www.webmd.com. Retrieved August 19, 2021, from https://www.webmd.com/vitamins/ai/ingredientmono-729/wormwood#:~:text=Seizure%20disorders%2C%20including%20epilepsy%3A%20Wormwood

webmd.com (2011). Echinacea: Uses, Side Effects, Interactions, Dosage, and Warning. Webmd.com. https://www.webmd.com/vitamins/ai/ingredientmono-981/echinacea

webmd.com (2019a). Hawthorn: Uses, Side Effects, Interactions, Dosage, and Warning. Webmd.com. https://www.webmd.com/vitamins/ai/ingredientmono-527/hawthorn

webmd.com (2019b). Panax Ginseng: Uses, Side Effects, Interactions, Dosage, and Warning. Webmd.com. https://www.webmd.com/vitamins/ai/ingredientmono-1000/panax-ginseng

Weeks, A (2011, August 17). Sage Tea & Pregnancy. Hello Motherhood. https://www.hellomotherhood.com/506957-sage-tea-pregnancy.html

Wei, J (2012, July 31). A Lovely Garden — Pink Lady Slipper and Native American Legends of the Ladyslipper (Cypripedeum Acaule). Eye on Life Magazine. https://eyeonlifemagazine.com/a-lovely-garden/pink-lady-slipper-and-native-american-legends-of-the-ladyslipper-cypripedeum-acaule#:~:text=Native%20peoples%20primarily%20used%20th

whatismyspiritanimal.com (n.d.). Buffalo Symbolism & Meaning | Spirit, Totem & Power Animal. What Is My Spirit Animal | Spirit, Totem, & Power Animals. Retrieved August 1, 2021, from https://whatismyspiritanimal.com/spirit-totem-power-animal-meanings/mammals/buffalo-bison-symbolism-meaning/#:~:text=The%20general%20meaning%20for%20Buffalo

Whelan, C (2019, May 9). Everything You Need to Know About Geranium Essential Oil. Healthline; Healthline Media. https://www.healthline.com/health/geranium-oil#benefits

wiki.medicinalplants-uses.com (n.d.). Townsendia - Encyclopedia of Medicinal Plants. Wiki.medicinalplants-Uses.com. Retrieved August 6, 2021, from https://wiki.medicinalplants-uses.com/index.php/Townsendia

wildflower.org (n.d.). Lady Bird Johnson Wildflower Center - The University of Texas at Austin. Www.wildflower.org. Retrieved August 17, 2021, from https://www.wildflower.org/plants/result.php?id_plant=LOIN

wildfoodsandmedicines.com/ (2014, May 1). Hawthorn. Wild Foods and Medicines. http://wildfoodsandmedicines.com/hawthorn/

williams.edu (2019). Creation Myths -- Iroquois Creation Myth. Williams.edu. https://www.cs.williams.edu/~lindsey/myths/myths_12.html

Wilson, D. R (2020, April 27). Echinacea: Benefits, uses, side effects, and effectiveness. Www.medicalnewstoday.com. https://www.medicalnewstoday.com/articles/252684#uses

wlegendsofamerica.com (2021, May). Medicine Wheel & the Four Directions – Legends of America. Www.legendsofamerica.com. https://www.legendsofamerica.com/na-medicinewheel/

wnps.org (n.d.). Arctostaphylos uva-ursi. Www.wnps.org. Retrieved August 6, 2021, from https://www.wnps.org/native-plant-directory/43-arctostaphylos-uva-ursi

Wolf, W (n.d.). Native American Hair Growth Secrets: 5 Hair Care Tips From the Elders. White Wolf. Retrieved August 6, 2021, from http://www.whitewolfpack.com/2015/04/native-american-hair-growth-secrets-5.html

Wong, C (n.d.). What Slippery Elm Can Help You With. Verywell Health. Retrieved August 12, 2021, from https://www.verywellhealth.com/the-benefits-of-slippery-elm-89585

wp.stolaf.edu (n.d.). Wild Ginger – Natural Lands. Wp.stolaf.edu. Retrieved August 9, 2021, from https://wp.stolaf.edu/naturallands/woodlands/ephemerals/wildginger/

xavier.edu (n.d.). Native American Prayers. Www.xavier.edu. Retrieved August 1, 2021, from https://www.xavier.edu/jesuitresource/online-resources/prayer-index/native-american#:~:text=Prayer%20of%20The%20Seven%20Directions

Images

Analogicus (n.d.). Yarrow. In figure 10. Retrieved August 24, 2021, from https://pixabay.com/photos/yarrow-wild-herbs-blossom-bloom-3571494/

AnnaER (n.d.). Purple Violets. In Figure 6. Retrieved August 24, 2021, from https://pixabay.com/photos/flowers-pansy-garden-violet-200270/

ChiemSeherin (n.d.). Hawthorne. In Figure 11. Retrieved August 24, 2021, from https://pixabay.com/photos/tree-branches-light-hawthorn-3637385/

congerdesign (n.d.). Mint Tea. In Figure 18. Retrieved August 24, 2021, from https://pixabay.com/photos/rhus-typhina-staghorn-sumac-846429/

Conscious Design (n.d.). Dried ginger and other herbs. In Figure 20. Retrieved August 24, 2021, from https://unsplash.com/photos/iSGbjKZ9erg

fotoblend (n.d.). wait-away-chicory-flower-plant. In figure 3. Retrieved August 24, 2021, from https://pixabay.com/photos/wait-away-chicory-flower-plant-6503204/

Free-Photos (n.d.). dreamcatcher-talisman-indian. In figure 1. Retrieved August 24, 2021, from https://pixabay.com/photos/dreamcatcher-talisman-indian-336639/

G, N (n.d.). bloodroot-sanguinaria-canadensis. In figure 2. Retrieved August 24, 2021, from https://pixabay.com/photos/bloodroot-sanguinaria-canadensis-1158978/

Hans (n.d.). Lavender flowers. In Figure 5. Retrieved August 24, 2021, from https://pixabay.com/photos/lavender-flowers-plants-field-1117275/

Hendry, P (2018). Mormon Tea. In Figure 14. https://unsplash.com/photos/3KwYVwqKwE8

jplenio (n.d.). Dandelion Closeup. In Figure 7. Retrieved August 24, 2021, from https://pixabay.com/photos/nature-dandelion-macro-close-up-3092555/

Kollegova, N (n.d.). The Lady's Slipper Orchid. In figure 4. Retrieved August 24, 2021, from https://pixabay.com/photos/the-lady-s-slipper-large-flowered-2489247/

Kukuts, I (n.d.). In Figure 8. Retrieved August 24, 2021, from https://pixabay.com/photos/echinacea-purpurea-echinacea-flower-4406439/

MabelAmber (n.d.). Green Briar. In Figure 19. Retrieved August 24, 2021, from https://pixabay.com/photos/rose-bush-rose-rose-hip-fruit-food-3050991/

manfredrichter (n.d.). Witch Hazel. In figure 9. Retrieved August 24, 2021, from https://pixabay.com/photos/witch-hazel-hamamelis-winterblueher-3137717/

MarcoRoosink (n.d.). Cattail Stalk. In Figure 15. Retrieved August 24, 2021, from https://pixabay.com/photos/cattail-loosestrife-stinky-cigar-526000/

RitaE (n.d.). Elderberry. In Figure 12. Retrieved August 24, 2021, from https://pixabay.com/photos/elder-elderberries-berry-juice-2652553/

Silviarita (n.d.). Ginger tea. In Figure 18. Retrieved August 24, 2021, from https://pixabay.com/photos/ginger-hot-lemon-tea-lemon-snow-1918107/

Tower, A (n.d.). Bear cub in an Uva Ursi bush. In Figure 13. Retrieved August 24, 2021, from https://pixabay.com/photos/bear-cub-black-head-eating-59535/

Wikimedia Images (n.d.). Rhus Typhinia. In Figure 17. Retrieved August 24, 2021, from https://pixabay.com/photos/rhus-typhina-staghorn-sumac-846429/

Made in the USA
Middletown, DE
24 June 2023